FROM MONKS TO MISSIONARIES

FROM MONKS *to* MISSIONARIES

Schools of Spirituality in the Christian Tradition

Nicki Verploegen

CASCADE *Books* • Eugene, Oregon

FROM MONKS TO MISSIONARIES
Schools of Spirituality in the Christian Tradition

Copyright © 2011 Nicki Verploegen. All rights reserved. Except for brief quotations in critical publications or reviews, no part of this book may be reproduced in any manner without prior written permission from the publisher. Write: Permissions, Wipf and Stock Publishers, 199 W. 8th Ave., Suite 3, Eugene, OR 97401.

Previously published in 2011 under the title *Legacy of the Founders: From Monks to Missionaries*

Cascade Books
An Imprint of Wipf and Stock Publishers
199 W. 8th Ave., Suite 3
Eugene, OR 97401

www.wipfandstock.com

ISBN 13: 978-1-62032-970-2

Cataloging-in-Publication data:

Verploegen, Nicki.

    From Monks to Missionaries : Schools of Spirituality in the Christian Tradition / Nicki Verploegen.

    xiv + 134 p. ; 23 cm. —

    ISBN 13: 978-1-62032-970-2

    1. Monasticism and religious orders. 2. Monastic and religious life. I. Title.

BX801 .V55 2011

Manufactured in the U.S.A.

This book is dedicated in gratitude to all the religious women and men who have offered me hospitality, welcome, and affirmation, most recently the Society of African Missions, the Maryknoll Missioners, the Spiritans, the Dominican Missionary Sisters in Zimbabwe and London, the Presentation Sisters of the Blessed Virgin Mary in Zimbabwe, the Little Children of the Blessed Lady in Zimbabwe, the SJI Sisters in Zimbabwe, the Missionaries of Charity of Zimbabwe, the RSHM Sisters in Zimbabwe, the Assumption Sisters of Nairobi, the Religious Sisters of Our Lady of the Missions in Kenya and Bangladesh, the Sisters of Charity of Cincinnati, the Redemptorists in Japan and the U.S., as well as those communities who have been most formative in my own spiritual path, the Jesuits, the Franciscans, the Sisters of Charity of Leavenworth, the Brothers of St. John of God, the Spanish Sisters of the Immaculate Conception and the Precious Blood Sisters in Liberia, West Africa, and Carmelite Sisters of Barrington, Rhode Island.

Contents

Acknowledgments ix

Introduction:
Schools of Spirituality in the Christian Tradition xi

PART I *Monastic Spirituality*

Introduction 3
1. Augustinian Spirituality: Hearts Aflame for the Trinity 7
2. Benedictine Spirituality: Christian Monastic Origins 15
3. Cistercians, Trappists, and Trappistines:
   Contemplatives in Community 23

PART II *Mendicant Spirituality*

Introduction 33
4. Franciscan Spirituality: Mendicants as Friars Minores 37
5. Dominican Spirituality: Friars Preachers of the Truth 45
6. Carmelite Spirituality: A Mendicant and Mystical Style 52

PART III *Ministerial and Active Apostolic Spirituality*

Introduction 63
7. Ignatian Spirituality: Spirituality in a World of Action 67
8. Redemptorist Spirituality: Preachers to the Populace 76
9. Salesian Spirituality:
   Living the Compassion of Jesus in Society 83
10. Marist Spirituality: A Marian Missionary Style 90

PART IV   *Missionary Spirituality*
         Introduction 99
    11   Spirituality of the Spiritans: Missionaries
         and Educators to the Poor and Abandoned 105
    12   Maryknoll Spirituality:
         Missionaries of Presence and Purpose 113
    13   Spirituality of the Society of African Missions:
         Dedication to Africa 122

         Epilogue 129

Acknowledgments

MANY PEOPLE'S INPUT GO into making a book. In this case the many lives of those who have inspired me throughout the centuries are the very meat of the text. Certainly, I must acknowledge the gift that these women and men have offered to make this text come to be. But then there are the specific women, men, and communities who have played a role in the germination of this work. I would like to thank Bob Heyer for initially contacting me to write a series for an electronic magazine with Liguori Publications and then urging me to let the book emerge from within that. Thank you to Dr. Edward Mahoney at St. Michael's College in Burlington, Vermont, who invited me to test the material with faculty and students in courses and seminars on schools of spirituality. Thank you to friends Fr. Paul Coury, CSSr, and Karen Duffy who were cheerleaders from the side. Lastly, thanks to Charlie Collier of Cascade Books for his editorial assistance, Heather Carraher for her typesetting work, and James Stock for his ongoing support.

Introduction

Schools of Spirituality in the Christian Tradition

"What kind of priest are you?" I queried. Fr. McCarthy looked dumbfounded. I was barely eighteen years of age and had just started my first semester at Carroll College, a small liberal arts diocesan college in Helena, Montana. "You know," I clarified, "are you a Jesuit or a Franciscan, or what?"

I smiled encouragingly. I was familiar with religious congregations. In rural Havre, Montana, where I was raised, St. Jude Thaddeus Church was a mission parish staffed by Jesuit priests and Franciscan sisters. These admirable priests and sisters had reared me in the faith. These were the only priests and nuns that I had known. So, innocently, I wanted to know to which religious community Fr. McCarthy belonged.

"I am a diocesan priest," he finally answered. That meant nothing to me so I inquired again. "Okay, but what community are you?" He now smiled. "I am a diocesan priest, ordained for the Helena diocese. That is my community." I had never heard of diocesan clergy. We were both startled. It was the beginning of my education beyond my parochial experience into a larger world in the church. I started to ask further questions around what were the distinctions between these. I wanted to know what the differences were between communities of religious and their origins, as well as this new category of diocesan clergy. This information would factor into my discernment about my own vocation, ministry, and call to serve.

Now looking back on it, I realize that the bulk of my formation as a Catholic Christian came from those early years of "schooling" by the religious communities with whom I prayed and lived as a child. It was at their

Introduction: Schools of Spirituality in the Christian Tradition

knees that I learned about developing a passionate relationship with God. In my experience, religious men and women were clustered around the genius of an early founder, who breathed inspiration and life into those who wanted to live their fire for God together. Though my knowledge as a child was rudimentary, I knew there were differences between these religious communities for the men and women who belonged to them.

St. Benedict was the first one to refer to religious communities as "schools of spirituality" through which one could learn about faith and discover how to express it more fully. A phenomenally rich heritage has been left to us by these religious communities, which have emerged throughout the centuries. As I have grown to appreciate the gifts of diocesan clergy, I have also recovered a profound respect and gratitude for these "schools of spirituality" formed over the centuries by religious women and men, which schooled me in the faith.

I circle back to those early days of exposure to priests, sisters, brothers, and lay associates who buzzed with attraction to the founders from which their communities were born. I knew the Second Vatican Council invited them to return to their founders to see if they needed to recapture some of that original fire that prompted them to start something new. I wanted to see what they still had to offer us. I wanted to know more about the founders of these "schools," the charism or specific spirit of these men and women, which formalized itself into structured communities so that generations of like-minded believers could follow in their footsteps.

Perhaps I am not alone in this quest for knowledge about different religious communities and their origins. Like me, you may be a little familiar with some of the schools of Christian spirituality and the orders that continue today. Perhaps you went to a school run by the Jesuits, the Dominicans, or the Franciscans. Maybe you have read literature produced by the Redemptorists or Carmelites or Maryknoll. You may have been intrigued by monastic buildings that you have seen and wondered about what a Benedictine or a Trappist is. Fundamentally, though, you do not know much about the development and identity of these congregations.

This book is an introduction to these "schools of spirituality" out of which has grown an amazing array of Catholic religious communities. These communities developed over centuries in response to real needs of people of faith. Terms like "monastic," "mendicant," "ministerial," or "missionary" may be somewhat new or ambiguous, but they are umbrella categories that describe forms of spirituality that broadened the

Introduction: Schools of Spirituality in the Christian Tradition

opportunities for people of faith to explore their devotion to God and serve the larger community. They continue today to be fabulous resources for our own development.

This book attempts to introduce these umbrella terms and the religious congregations that live out these styles of spirituality. The numerous founders and foundresses, whose energy formalized into "schools of spirituality" through the centuries, have stories and spiritualities with the power to enhance our own spiritual lives even today.

This book is divided into four parts. Each part opens with an introduction to a school of spirituality, a category such as monasticism, mendicancy, ministerial or active apostolic, and missionary. Following this brief description, individual religious congregations that incarnate this type of spirituality are explored. Like an umbrella, these religious communities form the "spokes" that make up the overarching school of spirituality as it has evolved through time to today. These communities offer a vivid illustration of the lived reality of this type of spirituality and how it shapes the religious identity of each group and offers us something now.

Since the founder is significant in the emergence of each "school," each chapter will include an overview of the historical time period in which the founder lived, followed by the founder's own story of call and response to God. Out of this, a description of the spiritual legacy bequeathed by the founder is outlined. Finally, pertinent for us today is a section on relevant spiritual and pastoral contributions this spiritual tradition continues to offer to contemporary Christians.

As believers in the twenty-first century, we are dependent on those who have gone before us to transmit the faith. Because they have bravely told their stories of struggle, fidelity, and failure, we can walk more easily in the Christian path. These stories through time have gathered idealistic followers that have institutionalized what they have learned so that it can be passed on more readily to the next body of believers. Their stories convince us that we, too, with all our beauty and blemishes, have a place in the building up of the faith. We stand on their shoulders and depend on their encouragement.

As we journey together, I hope you will enjoy the passage through history and add to your own knowledge of the origins of these schools and the women and men who have contributed to this storehouse of wisdom. Indeed, our story has been enriched and blessed by these feisty, controversial, and saintly sages whose radical choice to follow the Spirit lead them into new terrain and resulted in the emergence of a diversity of forms of spiritual lifestyles. From within the treasure house of Christian riches, we, then, can draw support and inspiration to contribute our own stories and pass on this legacy to those who come after.

PART I
Monastic Spirituality

Introduction

PERHAPS ONE OF THE most enduring schools of spirituality in Christianity is that of monasticism. This first umbrella category is alluring even for modern persons. Monasticism connotes a life of community, prayer, and haunting intimacy with God. Monasteries that are as ancient as the Christian faith itself mark our landscape, whispering invitations to come closer to God. They speak of stability, strength, and stillness.

Many Christians have a fundamental familiarity with the basics of monasticism. This form of spiritual life has endured many centuries of turmoil, trauma, and trouble and provided a safe harbor for people, manuscripts, and prayer. We associate monasticism with community and contemplation. It is traditionally seen as a conservative lifestyle that requires us to go away to a place dedicated to foundational practices of solitude, silence, and Scripture.

Within all the major religious traditions on the planet, monasticism is one of the oldest forms of spiritual life. Monastic life finds expression in many religious traditions like Buddhism, Hinduism, and others throughout the world. However, within Christianity, it was not always understood as a conservative lifestyle.

Monasticism emerged in the fourth century as a reaction against the institutionalization and alignment of Christianity with the Constantinian Empire. In 312 CE when the Edict of Milan brought Christians out of the catacombs to be embraced by the emperor as an acceptable and official state religion, a number of developments occurred. First of all, this acceptance and endorsement of Christianity freed curious seekers to investigate and join the previously hidden and threatened religion. Secondly, there was political and economic support for this inquiry. While many

Part I: Monastic Spirituality

joined the church with a true spiritual motivation, a large number joined with mercenary objectives. They could advance in their social position or political reputation by ascribing to Christianity. What resulted was a huge influx of poorly catechized members, who lacked the genuine fervor and devotion that previously had marked a church of martyrs and mystics, who had to fight and withstand great personal risk and condemnation.

Many zealous Christian souls saw this as a dampening of the original fire of Christ's Gospel message. In reaction against this contamination in the cities, they fled to desert places to try to recover a more radical way of honoring Christ. These desert dwellers recognized the need to embrace a life of ascetical discipline, centered on Scripture, simplicity, and silence. The desert was a harsh place that stripped people of the securities and illusions behind which they could hide. From a spiritual perspective, the desert provided an environment for naked dependence on God, a radical return to what was essential: God and God's providence.

But it also was a dangerous place. These Desert Abbas and Ammas realized a need to stay connected with each other in order to survive. Some gathered together in small clusters, living within view of each other but living lives as hermits. Others chose to live together under a common roof with a Rule to guide their communal life.

Out of this latter development, monasticism emerged. The various Rules of life that were formulated as a result of experimentation by different groups and individuals dictated a balanced lifestyle of prayer, work, and study. A basic daily rhythm that revolved around the liturgical cycle was composed of established times for communal prayer of the psalms and reflection on the writings of the Church Fathers. This balanced life of prayer governed those who joined these ascetic communities. To broaden their intellects and inspire them spiritually, a regimen of study was incorporated into the schedule of each day. Finally, daily manual labor helped ground these monastics in the earth and allowed time for the agriculture needed to provide for their material needs. They maintained self-sufficiency and often provided a livelihood for local populations who sprang up around them and linked themselves economically and spiritually to those praying within the walls of the monastery.

Monastic communities in Christianity began to flourish in the fifth century CE and became further structured by great men and women who reflected on their experience and adapted Rules to guide the healthy spiritual life in their communities. Monasteries grew as centers of learning, copying manuscripts before printing presses were invented. In the Dark Ages when invasions threatened the populace, monasteries became places of sanctuary, safeguarding refugees within their walls and preserving artifacts and precious objects from destruction. Eventually, they were places that housed the riches of the church and the society.

Monasticism is a form of spirituality that uses structured formal prayer in a communal setting, usually apart from populated areas. The routine of life is grounded in an apostolate of prayer. In other words, their prayer is their work. Community and prayer are the centerpieces of a monastic's life. Monks and monastic nuns commit themselves to lives of stability, never leaving the original monastery that they first joined unless a new foundation requires them to do so. Enclosed and restricted by their communal rhythm, monks and nuns of monastic communities display the high value they place on communal life. The monastic buildings which house their lives provide an image of the stability of faith that has survived many generations of change.

Today, we continue to relish the soothing, mystical chanting of prayer that comes out of this ancient spiritual tradition and we find nourishment for our souls in the refuge of monasteries and churches surrounding them. In the following chapters let us explore three communities of monastic men and women, the Augustinians, the Benedictines, and the Cistercians or Trappists and the Trappistines to see how this style of spirituality diversified creatively according to various needs through the ages.

1

Augustinian Spirituality
Hearts Aflame for the Trinity

"Late have I loved you, O Beauty ever ancient, ever new, late have I loved you! You were within me, but I was outside, and it was there that I searched for you." These words echo the ache of love that was a refrain in the heart of St. Augustine, the man from whom this school of spirituality gets its name. The poesy of these words reverberates through Augustine's writings, particularly in his *Confessions* where he tells the story of his conversion from a life of seeking love in the outside world to that of finding love in intimacy with God.

Augustinian spirituality can be characterized as both monastic and mendicant in its form. From this perspective, the spirituality of the Augustinian legacy is a combination and has witnessed resurgences throughout history of the same vigor manifest in the founder himself. Therefore, we return to the earliest days of the Christian formation story and include Augustinian spirituality in this first chapter, positioning its inception in the era of the founder. In this milieu we discover the elements that powerfully influenced his spiritual formation and the school of spirituality to which his name would eventually be attached.

Part I: Monastic Spirituality

The Milieu

It was the late 300s CE. Persecution of Christianity had been halted just over forty years prior, in 312 CE, with Constantine's conversion in the Eastern end of the Roman Empire. Many ecclesial and governmental issues were still being hammered out. Schisms had occurred within Christianity, challenging the authority of bishops, who had apostasized or betrayed their Christian faith during the persecution. Theological battles began over the true meaning of Christ's life. Heresies developed with controversies over what composed orthodox belief.

In Northern Africa the Donatist heretics raised a question about the authenticity of the sacraments presided at by those who were weak of faith. They replaced the appointed prelates with those whom they felt manifested greater fidelity to the martyrs they wanted continually to honor. Initially, the official response to this was to turn a blind eye, but eventually suppression was implemented and, sadly, civil wars resulted.

These theological wars occurred at the same time as barbarian invasions from the north, and collectively they compromised the stability of Roman governance in the West. In Northern Africa a weakened centralized government struggled with cultural diversity at the edge of the Christian world.

Augustine's birthplace was Thagaste, North Africa, what is now modern day Algeria. This city was host to a mixture of religious cultures, theological attitudes, and spiritual practices. Paganism was equally strong within the vestige of what remained of a viable Roman outpost. Thagaste was decidedly Christian by the time of Augustine's birth, but the heretical influence of the Donatists was ensconced in the ritual practices and martyr cults of the local people.

The Founder

Into this turbulent and provocative scene, Augustine (354–430 CE) was born to middle-class parents, a Christian mother, Monica, who eventually was declared the patron saint of mothers and wives, and a pagan father named Patricius. Augustine was given as many advantages as his family and the patronage of a wealthy townsman could afford, including a classical education in Greek (which he hated) and Latin (which he loved). With the support of a pagan priest, Romanian, he went on for graduate studies in Carthage after secondary school. Teaching would take him back to Thagaste, and also to Carthage. From there he would travel to Rome and Milan, where he would convert to the Catholic faith in 386 CE under the tutelage of the great St. Ambrose, being baptized in 387 CE. His mother's prayers would be answered in that sacramental moment, but she would die the same year en route to Africa with Augustine at her side.

Augustine's Christian life took him into monasticism, ministry, priesthood, and finally leadership as the Bishop of Hippo. He experimented with communal life, too, by living with companions in a monastic setting. Even after his ascendancy to the office of Bishop, he continued this monastic life with clerical colleagues, advocating for a renunciation of all private property and emphasizing charity and service. He would oversee his sister's monastic community and establish a monastic community of laymen. He would refute the heretical errors of his day through writing, preaching, and arbitration.

Within his lifetime, Augustine would see the political stability, which he took for granted in the Christian Roman Empire, crumble before him and eventually threaten his life. In 430 CE another heretical group, the "Arian" Christian Visigoths, besieged Hippo, cutting it off from the sea, and Augustine died during that siege at age seventy-six.

What Augustine provided in the midst of chaos within the church was a form of order, a systematic apologetic or explanation of Christianity to the heretical factions of his day, which included Manicheanism, Donatism, Pelagianism, and Arianism. His conversion to Christianity was a coming home to God, a Trinity of Father, Son, and Holy Spirit, where his joy and passion could be most fully realized. This return on Augustine's part included not just an intellectual endorsement of the kingdom of God, but an active consent to helping that kingdom be established on earth. Through a self-transcending love of God and of other persons, the city of God would come to be.

A Spiritual Legacy for Today:
Caritas in Relationship to God and World

Augustine lived at a time of intense ecclesial, social, and political stress. Contemporaries of his include St. Ambrose (340–397 CE), whose talent for leadership in the Roman model provided support for self-rule for the

Part I: Monastic Spirituality

Catholic Church, St. Jerome (347–420 CE), whose learned abilities in Greek and Latin were used for some of the first scriptural translations and commentaries, St. Benedict (480–547 CE), who introduced a new monasticism that provided stability and moral order in the chaos of broken political structures, and St. Patrick (392–461 CE), one of the first missionary-monks who carried Christianity to Ireland. The contributions that Augustine made, however, to the theological and spiritual literature we have today merit his designation as a Doctor of the Church. Let us look now at this heritage that Augustine bequeathed to future generations through *caritas*, his devotion to the Trinity, his encouragement of a deep personal relationship with God, and his advocacy for personal transformation that can lead to transformation of the world.

Caritas

Augustine brought with himself a life challenged by struggle and choice. His legacy is a call to choose a love that can carry us through difficulty into devotion. Augustine provided a philosophical and theological basis from which monasticism could be built. His contribution was less about the structure of monasticism, which Benedict would later bring to his school of spirituality, but more about the foundational spiritual principles of charity and faith that undergird healthy Christian communal life.

Augustine's legacy to the theological and spiritual world was love or "caritas." *Caritas* was a central theme in Augustinian spirituality, indicating that a change in the direction of the way we love is required in the spiritual life. This emphasis on love had implications for the believer. There was a radical passion involved in this understanding of relationship with God. Augustine's teachings promoted a spirituality that had intellectual, moral, ministerial, and mystical implications. His writings in their poetic form reveal a soul deeply enraptured by God, a restless soul who had come home.

The Trinity

Central to Augustine's spirituality was the image of the Trinity, through whom we are called to reform our lives by the grace of Christ and enter into friendship with God. Augustine was so enamored with the Trinity that he wrote fifteen books about the Father, Son, and Holy Spirit. Trinitarian theology was still relatively new within Christian thought in the late fourth century and Augustine championed this image of God as relational and loving. In a time of serious heretical questioning about Christ as God and man, he ardently wrote of Christ as the perfect image of God in communion with God, as a human being. He wrote that this was the most basic understanding for a Christian in explaining their experience of God. Foundational to the Christian life was this conviction and commitment to engagement with the Trinity.

The Development of a Personal Relationship with God

There was passion in the spirituality of Augustine. It radiated with fervent religious sentiment for God. Augustine invited people to seek wisdom through relationship with the triune God. This was not based on a remote sense of God. Rather, a personal intimacy with God the Father through Christ was required of the Christian, whose movement into intimacy would be infused gradually by the Holy Spirit. This infusion guides the person towards perfection of a life of holiness. Love thus forms the person into the image of Christ. This was *caritas* in its ideal form, something Augustine encouraged all Christians to embrace and incorporate into their spiritual lives.

Personal Transformation and the World

This conversion process was not exclusive to the individual human being. The implication of true conversion was witnessed in active participation in the transformation of the world through love and peacemaking. Certainly, Augustine's modeling of peacemaking inspired and won back many persons who were grappling with heretical positions. His compassionate approach, his skillful use of rhetoric, and his intellectual clarity convinced numerous hearers of the validity of his position and brought them back into union with the larger Christian community. Applicable today, his articulate passion for communion with God arouses hearts who want to identify themselves with love and collaborate in the re-creation of the world.

Part I: Monastic Spirituality

Contemporary Spiritual and Pastoral Contributions

Augustine's contribution to the spiritual and theological world is admittedly immense. While many translators have interpreted Augustine's work with decidedly negative overtones with regard to sexuality, women, and marriage, the magnitude of what he wrote cannot be refuted. He defended Christianity in a chaotic era, when little guidance was available through the structures we assume today. Of note to contemporary Christians is Augustine's introduction of a new literary genre—the spiritual autobiography—the notion of the conversion process as gradual, and the recovery of love and forgiveness as theological virtues.

Spiritual Autobiography

St. Augustine introduced a new form of literary reflection in the book of his life, *The Confessions of St. Augustine*. In his candid self-disclosure, he modeled a reflective approach to reviewing his life in relation to himself, his God, and other persons. He told his story, complete with the stumbling and mumblings through which he tried to find meaning. He discovered God. This example gives us permission to look back on our own story and revisit it through the eyes of faith.

Since his time, many other formative writers have offered similar accounts of their own journeys, i.e., Teresa of Avila's *The Life*, Therese Lisieux's *The Story of a Soul*, Thomas Merton's *Seven Storey Mountain*. Many contemporary researchers in spirituality and psychology are discovering that a "narrative" approach to their work helps persons significantly in spiritual direction and therapy. A storytelling process allows people to articulate and preserve a sense of their meaning-making process as a person and the Spirit can manifest more profoundly in their everyday life events with this heightened self-awareness.

The Conversion Process as Gradual

Counter to contemporary attempts to achieve perfection instantaneously, Augustinian spirituality reminds us that the conversion process is an ongoing one, gradually developed by degrees. Under the influence of the Holy Spirit, we progressively ascend to God in intimacy. That intimacy is inaugurated and sustained by God's initiative. Most effectively, our conversion occurs when our will complies with God's movement. Therefore, we stand in dependency upon God, not on our own cleverness. We will not move deeper into intimacy with God through a systematic series of intellectual steps, techniques, or philosophical assertions. A virtuous life must be practiced daily, and conversion will gradually be evidenced within a life of regular prayer, fasting, and submission to Christ the Physician, who heals all alienations.

Love and Forgiveness as Theological Virtues

Vatican II recovered an emphasis on many of the theological virtues that had been deemphasized through ages of conflict, fear, and defensiveness. One focus that was recovered finds its roots in the emphasis on love and forgiveness within Augustinian spirituality. From the Augustinian perspective, the purpose of all acts of self-denial or ascetical discipline was to increase one's love of God and others. But this connection had been overshadowed for many centuries by an experience of asceticism that was cheerless and dour. Many experienced the liturgical season of Lent as a time of loveless repentance, laden with heavy self-recrimination. The sense of love behind the purgative practices was lost.

The restoration of the value of love as the original emphasis of Lent reflects an Augustinian influence. Stemming from this is the Augustinian charism of forgiveness. The capacity to forgive and receive forgiveness is at the heart of an Augustinian monk's life. In today's age, forgiveness is a virtue sorely needed in practice and in reception. Forgiving self, as well as forgiving others, is an essential mandate from Christ that stretches us beyond our pettiness, our narrow perspectives, and our preferences. Forgiveness, one of the most challenging principles of Christianity, is foundational to the conversion of the individual Christian and the transformation of a troubled world.

In Summary

Depicted often in artistic renditions as a man holding a heart in flames, St. Augustine carries the association of a person who struggled passionately with his interior life and external lifestyle. Down through the centuries countless men and women have resonated with Augustine's desire for spiritual intimacy with God. The Rule of St. Augustine is the oldest surviving rule for religious in the Western world and models itself after the motto of "union with others in a common love of God."

The Rule has served as the anchor for hundreds of religious communities, monastic, mendicant, and apostolic, since the early fifth century. Some of the men's groups include: The Order of St. Augustine, the Canons Regular, the Premonstratensians, the Servites, and the Assumptionists. Discalced Augustinians also emerged in the sixteenth century along with the Augustinian Recollects in the 1900s. Some women's groups which espouse Augustinian spirituality include the Bridgettines, the Annunciates, the Ursulines, the Angelicals of St. Paul, the Sisters of Our Lady of Charity of Refuge, the Daughters of the Good Shepherd, Salesian Sisters, and the Poor Teaching Sisters of our Blessed Lady.

Laity, too, have benefited from St. Augustine's rich legacy. He never defined a spirituality specific to laity but recognized the level of charity as the distinguishing characteristic of a more effective Christian life. Religious, laity, and clergy were all about one thing: building up the Body of Christ and reflecting that in the renovation of the world. In Augustinian spirituality, no life should be too busy so as not to pray, nor should leisure be too extensive as to not afford charitable action towards one's neighbor. Love was always the underlying element. Fuse one's life with the heart of Christ, and then, informed by that love, "love and do what you will."

Questions for Reflection:

- Have you ever experienced that ache of love that Augustine did?
- Did it move you somehow towards God?
- When you look at your own spiritual story, do significant events emerge as pivotal in your life of faith?

Resources for Ongoing Study:

St. Augustine. *The Confessions of St. Augustine*. Translated by John K. Ryan. Garden City, NY: Doubleday, 1960.
Brown, Peter. *Augustine of Hippo: A Biography*. 2nd ed. Berkeley: University of California Press, 2000.
Wills, Garry. *Saint Augustine*. New York: Penguin, 1999.

2

Benedictine Spirituality
Christian Monastic Origins

No one can speak of monasticism as a school of spirituality without directly linking it to the figure of St. Benedict of Nursia. Our use of the phrase "schools of spirituality" originated with Benedict who viewed the monastery as a school for spiritual development. The milieu in which he lived and crafted the monastic life was one that was filled with chaos in Western Europe. The school of spirituality that his genius created has become the cornerstone for the majority of monastic communities worldwide within Christianity. Monasticism in the West took its decided shape from the phenomenal leadership of Benedict of Nursia.

The Milieu

As mentioned in the introduction to monasticism, for all its staid characteristics, monasticism was not always so structured and stable. Some scholars would situate the origins of monasticism in the Egyptian deserts of the fourth century, when devout laymen and women escaped the sociopolitical conventions and mediocrity of a Christianity that had emerged from hiding with its acceptance as a state religion. In an attempt to recapture the radicalism of the martyrs, desert abbas and ammas adopted

Part I: Monastic Spirituality

austere lives of solitude and asceticism. Gradually, these individuals gathered into clusters and attempted to live communally.

The monastic lifestyle that Benedict came into in the late 400s was filled with roaming monks without supervision or spiritual guidance. True order and discipline was missing from their lives. Benedict's contribution to monasticism was providing for the monks assembled with him a stable and balanced approach to a prayerful life in common. The legislative genius of the Benedictine way was so profound that the way of life he proffered was embraced by monastics throughout Europe within decades after Benedict's death.

The Founder

St. Benedict of Nursia (480–547 CE), known as "the Father of Europe," was born of an affluent family in Italy and studied in Rome. At a young age, Benedict became appalled by the paganism he witnessed. He saw a Christianity that was crumbling in the city and he felt he must retreat into the life of a hermit near Subiaco in order to live a genuine faithful life. He fled society to live a solitary life in a cave. It appears he underwent a deep religious conversion and news spread that here was a holy man. He was sought out by monks to become their leader. Initially friendly with him, these followers later turned against him and tried to poison him. Leaving that group, he later was found by another and he accepted leadership there. These disciples, who gathered around him, helped him found the monastery of Monte Cassino along with numerous others.

The era in which Benedict lived was fraught with political instability with the sacking of Rome and the wars between rivaling barbarian tribes. Perhaps Benedict's talent for order was a gift of the Holy Spirit to the disorder of the times. The severe austerity that he had practiced as a hermit softened into a more balanced form. From his personal experience as a spiritual searcher and leader, St. Benedict wrote for his monks *The Rule* that applied some structure, moderation, and depth in a meaningful way to the communal life at the monastery. Through the practices assembled in *The Rule*, individuals could attain virtue and sanctify all of their life to God.

The stability that Benedict introduced to monastic life produced an atmosphere conducive for a life focused on personal sanctification and the sacred. No mention of an apostolate can be found in *The Rule*. Benedict knew the nature of humanity and recognized that the habitual application in daily life of ritual, prayer, and charity would be difficult for many. Yet, he issued the challenge to his monks to empty themselves of self-will and selfishness and dwell in love with their brothers. In the routine of living together, God would be found.

To curb the restlessness so prevalent in his day, Benedict required the monks to take a vow of stability, promising to remain in the same enclosure the duration of their monastic life. The monastery then became a self-supporting, self-contained community with no outside authority. The abbot was comparable to the bishop in status and was the primary governing figure.

Fixed times of prayer in common and in private were primary. Four hours daily were devoted to liturgical worship, another four hours to private reading and six hours to work with the hands. Silence permeated the atmosphere. This structure provided the necessary foundation for earnest souls seeking God to flourish. It also was the stabilizing environment for unruly aspirants to tame their hearts so that God could work in them.

Spiritual Legacy for Today: Guidance for an Ordering of Life

When we inquire about the legacy that Benedict left us, we may balk at the highly structured lifestyle that is involved in the routine of a monastic community. Yet, in Benedict's day as in our own, such structure had value in the midst of great chaos and brokenness.

An ordered life cannot be assumed. Even the most intelligent of persons may find areas of disorder and ambiguity. Benedict's guidelines for living a holy life involved the combination of community, moderation, humble obedience, and vocal prayer. This emphasis in Western monasticism was in contrast to the individualistic, angelic, and competitive asceticism of monasteries in the Byzantine East. It grounded the monks of the West practically in a balanced life of work and study. We shall examine each of these elements that are part of the vast legacy left behind by Benedict of Nursia.

Part I: Monastic Spirituality

Community

Today many young people who come from broken homes and a fractured society crave the stability and tranquility of an ordered life. They long for a stable community through which they can touch the sacred. Such was the case in many of the wandering souls in Benedict's day who sought out a place in which they could feel God's presence.

While cloistered monasticism may be limited in its appeal, the lessons offered from it greatly benefitted the seeker who sincerely wanted to incorporate prayer, meditation, and a contemplative rhythm into their life. The habit of regular prayer, study, and labor within a community of peers, elders, and aspirants was a great support to those attempting to develop in the spiritual life. The community itself became a laboratory, a petri dish if you will, through which the experiment in spiritual maturation occurred. This environment proved an essential element for monks and nuns in the fostering of a contemplative focus. An individual respectful of leadership and the larger need of the community was both stretched and stabilized by the living ambiance that the community offered.

Moderation

Benedict's simple dictums in *The Rule* provided a regular daily schedule that balanced the life of work, reading, and worship under a common roof. It supplied guidance through simple methods. These methods required diligence and humility. Through faith, good works, and the guidance of the Gospel, Benedict encouraged his monks to reach for the goal of obedience, "to merit to see him who has called us into his kingdom."

Moderation governed the monastery. Benedict knew the hazards of excessive asceticism, isolation, activity, and laxity. His recommendation was for a moderate integration of the different facets of life. Work was necessary in order to eat. Study broadened the mind and heart. Prayer maintained the focus and contact with God and the inner self. All of these elements in moderation provided a proper balance and fostered holiness of life.

Obedience

Obedience to the abbot was essential. But the abbot's obedience to the Spirit was a very serious matter, as well. Given the feudal context of Benedict's era, a hierarchical approach was to be expected. But obedience implied a listening to the spirit and trusting that God was using the abbot to further the monk's movement into sanctity.

Surprising to us may be Benedict's invitation to see God in the least likely, the humblest of guests, the youngest of novices, the poorest wayfarer. All carried the richness of God. Special attention was given to each of these persons for through these one was often surprised by God and reminded of the unassuming ways in which God reveals God's self.

Vocal Prayer

The regular recitation aloud of the Psalms accompanied by a life of obedience in listening to the Holy Spirit had a formative influence in its regularity and focus. Verbal prayer spoken in common steeped the community in reminders for living an upright life of care and compassion. The Psalms were a vehicle for catechetical instruction. Gradually through repetition, the verses became memorized and integrated into the heart of the person praying. The Scripture was encountered in the liturgical life of the entire body of the community and reinforced in private devotion and prayer. Simple scripturally-based vocal prayer provided a discipline that enriched and grounded a person's life.

Contemporary Spiritual and Pastoral Contributions

When we examine the many spiritual gifts passed on to us through the tradition of St. Benedict, three obvious contributions come to mind. Guidance for a daily time of private, personal prayer and study is found in the transmission of the practice of Lectio Divina. A scripturally-based order of communal prayer for the hours of the day is seen in the Liturgy of the Hours. A structured lifestyle that maximizes the development of the interior life in common with others in an enclosed environment is the gift of monasticism.

Part I: Monastic Spirituality

Monasticism

Monasticism is a vocation not suited to everyone. But even today in the industrializing society in which we live, monasticism offers us an alternative to chaotic existence. An enclosed life, focused on a balanced rhythm of prayer, work, and study, monasticism is a way of life valued in many other religious traditions. It holds a privileged place in Christianity.

Benedict's gift was to standardize the daily regimen and offer guidance for living a life dedicated to God and contemplation. Benedict's *Rule* gave consistency and order to a rather freestyle existence for monks in his age. It provides the same for us and it has been time-tested over centuries of practice. Monasticism is one form of spiritual life that continues to invite people to depth and single-mindedness. Whether time in a monastery is a lifetime or a short time, monasticism has a viability that reminds us concretely that there is another way to live our lives, one that is specifically and unequivocally focused on God and the small community. This is a gift which has incomparable benefit, whether we frequent the space or not.

Lectio Divina

Lectio Divina is a classical monastic practice of prayerful reading of the Bible and reflecting contemplatively upon its meaning and instruction. While Lectio is not Bible study, it involves the reading of a Bible text in such a way as to open the reader to the Holy Spirit. It is practice that can be integrated outside the walls of a monastery as well as within.

In the monastic form of Lectio Divina, the individual prays with a text of Scripture and notices when there is movement within, prompted by a specific phrase in the text. This felt movement or quiver inside invites the reader to return to the phrase and dwell with it, repeating it slowly over and over again, letting it penetrate to the interior of the person of prayer. Lingering with the text opens the one who prays to new depth in the text. This prolonged listening to the word is not to analyze the text or understand it logically as much as to remain with it. New insights and meanings may also emerge for the person at prayer to integrate. Decidedly contemplative, Lectio Divina fosters a more receptive way of attending and learning from the Word.

Liturgy of the Hours

The Liturgy of the Hours is known also as "The Divine Office" or "The Breviary." In monasticism, the entire day is consecrated through vocal prayer. The community stops working at fixed times of the day and pauses for the Word of God. This practice draws the attention of the person at prayer to God through the recitation of Scripture and Psalms at regulated time periods during the day.

The recitation of the Liturgy of the Hours several times a day (monks do it five or six times) familiarizes a person with the many Psalms, instructions, and stories of Scripture, as well as the writings of the early Church. This recitation done habitually allows the words and ideas to sink in deeply and eventually erupt in the heart of the reader. Phrases rise up that comfort the person in times of suffering, provide inspiration in times of despair, and proclaim joy in times of celebration. The practice of prayer with the Bible, structured for us in the breviary-cycle, reinforces our knowledge of the texts and they gradually become an echo of our own interiors.

In Summary

Throughout the world Benedictine monasteries exist in great number for those attracted to contemplative stillness. Ministries of prayer, retreat, research, and writing have developed from within the Benedictine tradition. Universities, houses of prayer, and centers devoted to spiritual healing have moved contemporary Benedictine men and women into a greater apostolic thrust in the last century. Many laypeople associate with and affiliate themselves with specific communities to support their own practice of moderation. Some join the Benedictine family as oblates and further devote themselves to the Benedictine values and lifestyle as they continue to live their lives outside the walls of the monastery.

The principles generated within Benedict's communities serve many outside the monastic walls. The balance of prayer, communal life, work, and study is a model for anyone who wants to be healthy and mature spiritually. As places of prayer and worship, Benedictine houses continue to remind us of a transcendent reality and encourage a faithfulness that is as solid as the sixteen centuries that Benedictine spirituality has been in existence.

Part I: Monastic Spirituality

Questions for Reflection:

- Have you ever found yourself attracted to the monastery?
- What attracted you?
- Would you characterize your life as "an ordered life"?

Resources for Ongoing Study:

Fry, Timothy, editor. *The Rule of St. Benedict In English*. Collegeville, MN: Liturgical, 1982.

Gannon, Thomas M., and George W. Traub. *The Desert And The City: An Interpretation of the History of Christian Spirituality*. London: Macmillan, 1969.

3

Cistercians, Trappists, and Trappistines
Contemplatives in Community

SEVERAL TIMES WITHIN THE history of the church, a charism that led to the foundation of one school of spirituality would diversify in its form in later centuries, resulting in the development of a new form of religious life. A recovery of the original genius from which the community emerged may have been needed. A reform may have evolved that was an appropriate response to the needs of the current times. As the saying goes, one good thing led to another.

Such was the case with the founding of the Cistercian Order. The Cistercian Order, whose name comes from the mother abbey of Citeaux in France, was a reform of traditional Benedictine monasticism in the eleventh century. Centuries later, the Trappists developed as a reform within the Cistercian community in the early 1800s and became known as the Cistercian Order of the Strict Observance (O.C.S.O.). The Trappistines emerged as the female counterpart within this monastic family.

The Cistercians, Trappists, and Trappistines were all monastic communities whose interest was in a recovery of a radical poverty within their communal existence. The hunger for God was primary. This was to be lived out in fraternal communities that worked, ate, and prayed together. Let us look at the shifts in history that prompted these new developments.

Part I: Monastic Spirituality

The Milieu

After a long period of political maneuvering by powerful emperors, complicated by strife in the Eastern and Western religious debates, the church in the West, which had been in decline, began a slow recovery of strength and centralization in the 1100s. With the signing in 1122 CE of the Concordat of Worms, the church affirmed its right to elect bishops and abbots from within its ranks, rather than succumbing to political appointments by political sovereignties. With this new stability, a plethora of new religious endeavors occurred. A revival of interest in philosophical studies, the fathers of the church, and new theological thought supported the development of many great minds and spiritual leaders. New orders began to flourish and reforms within established communities were endorsed.

The Founders

The Founders of Cistercian spirituality were leaders and visionaries. Early in the eleventh century, a reform movement within monasticism, inaugurated by Pope Gregory VII, addressed the prosperity housed within the great monasteries of Europe. Within the Benedictine abbey at Citeaux, reform involved a return to the initial impulse that spawned it: a regard for poverty, a return to a more austere lifestyle, and an affirmation of moving away from worldly enterprises to focus on God.

Out of this concern for the integrity of Benedict's *Rule*, a new foundation called Citeaux was founded from Molesme, France, in 1098 CE. Branching off from this foundation, a small band of monks under the leadership of a series of abbots like Abbot Robert, Prior Alberic, and St. Stephen Harding began a new life in the "wilderness," twenty kilometers from Dijon, France.

The new foundation embraced a life of ascetical discipline, doing penance in expiation for sin. They chose to live in isolation, keeping their relations to a minimum and owning no property except what was needed to sustain the community. The rural atmosphere was desirable for their agricultural projects and they systematically transformed unarable land into gardens and farmland for their sustenance. Simplicity of life was maintained in an environment devoid of ornamentation and their ritual life was a radically simple liturgical rhythm without flourish.

Throughout history, these continued to be the mainstays of the hundreds of houses around the world, which fall under the Cistercian name. Simplicity, prayer, and communal life with a heremitical bent characterized the life of a Cistercian monk or Trappistine nun.

Spiritual Legacy for Today: Silence in a World of Noise

The legacy of the Cistercians and Trappists and Trappistines can best be described as one that fosters silence and stillness, encourages personal holiness, and models collegial governance. The bare-bones spirituality of the Cistercians and Trappists leaves little chance for external distraction that could derail the foundational focus of the man or woman within its walls. Let us reflect on this legacy of Citeaux.

Silence and Stillness

Throughout all ages the atmosphere of silence and stillness fostered within the monastic walls of Cistercians, Trappists, and Trappistines was a hallmark of the spirituality of this community. The environment of quiet within these monasteries refreshed souls. These practices were long identified as crucial for spiritual composure and inner preparation to meet the Divine. Monastics knew well the benefits of surrounding themselves with the quiet. Essential to the movement into depth was this still silent framework for their lives. Cistercian spirituality championed this practice within its monastic walls. Conversation was restricted in order that the monk or nun could completely give themselves over to the Spirit.

A part of the rich legacy bequeathed to subsequent generations was this invitation to come into the sanctuary of quiet and drink deep of its nourishment. Throughout history, visitors too had relished the sanctuary of silence that they found when they entered into the cloister of the Cistercian or Trappistine communities. This was a way of life that eliminated unnecessary noise that could prove a distraction to the real focus on God.

Personal Holiness

The Golden Age of Cistercian history from 1098 to 1250 CE produced many spiritual masters and saints, who wrote treatises on the path to personal holiness. Most noteworthy were St. Bernard of Clairvaux, William of Saint Thierry, and Aelred of Rievaulx, all of whom contributed masterful works on the spiritual life, prayer, and the call to holiness. These men through their mystical captivation by God described the journey of faith that led them into single-minded devotion. Their writings offered rich guidelines for the development of deep spiritual friendship with God.

They also wrote about the benefit of relationships with others of mature faith. Using their own experience of spiritual growth, they encouraged others on the path of holiness, often using vivid metaphors and images that stirred the reader. In so doing, they left a rich reservoir of literary masterpieces from which earnest seekers throughout the centuries have found inspiration and increased their own development.

Collegial Governance

Equally genius was the governing system that emerged from within the ranks of the Cistercian and Trappist communities. Leadership was maintained not exclusively by an individual abbot but by a chapter of abbots who met annually to collectively assess the state of the order. As co-abbots, they agreed to a united approach to the reform, committing to live in charity under a single rule with the same usage of various practices. The abbot of the founding monastery was very influential, but the chapter of co-abbots allowed them to join autonomous monasteries in one order, providing incredible stability and breadth of vision from within while allowing for some freedom within each house.

This method of governance would become the template for subsequent religious communities from the twelfth century on. This form was a novel approach to collegial decision-making with a respect for the autonomy of each monastic house. It provided checks and balances of authority, allowed for consultation, and provided continuity between individual communities. The forum allowed for discernment on the ongoing development of the charism or primal gift of the community and the regularity of communal life.

Contemporary Spiritual and Pastoral Contributions

One of the most paradoxical contributions that the Trappist community offers contemporary persons is the gift of one of its own, a monk called Father Louis, who touches millions under his identity as Thomas Merton. Situated in the provocative era from the 1940s to the 1960s, Merton's writings address many major social issues such as war, civil disobedience, the escalation of technology, and the media. His perspective is a unique one written from his hermitage in Kentucky.

Equally invested in the development of interior peace as well as the promulgation of international peace, Merton challenges people to rethink their spiritual, religious, and political assumptions. His writings transcend national and religious boundaries, reaching out ecumenically to Christians from all walks of life. Intrigued by Eastern monasticism and prayer, he offers rare insight into social issues that typically one does not associate as a concern for someone from a monastic enclosure.

Thomas Merton in his final days was traveling as a pilgrim, exploring the interface between Eastern and Western contemplative practice. On December 10, 1968, after addressing an inter-monastic forum in Bangkok, his life ended through accidental electrocution from a faulty fan. What are the spiritual and pastoral contributions that the Trappist, Thomas Merton, makes to contemporary persons? We will explore three, namely, autobiographical example, contemplative hunger, and transformation of the human person and society.

Autobiographical Example

An account of Merton's own process of conversion and reflection is chronicled in his countless books, letters, and articles. His profoundly personal autobiographical account of his life is a bestseller under the title, *The Seven Storey Mountain*. Not unlike the masterful autobiography of St. Augustine, this too is the story of a man who grapples with his own choices, his vulnerabilities, and his passions. His exceptional wit and refreshing candor make this book a must-read for people shaped by industrializing society and technological culture.

From Merton, we realize that it is helpful to reflect upon and to tell our own story to see the hand of God played out in the folds of our experience. We learn about God's invitations through the foibles and frailty of being human. This is all a part of the spiritual life. It is in reflecting on that experience that wisdom can grow. Merton gives us permission in his modeling of self-disclosure to examine the circuitous routes God often takes to draw us closer. Whether the autobiographical process is one that is written or spoken, we discover the value in unpacking our own histories so that the patterns and pitfalls that make up our personalities can be squarely acknowledged and addressed.

Contemplative Hunger

For contemporary persons, Merton brings contemplation out of the monastery onto center stage. Prayer in the center of one's person is no longer relegated to convents and monasteries. It is a practice that is validated as appropriate for any earnest seeker, regardless of vocational distinctions, economic status, or religious affiliation. Merton teaches us about prayer using contemporary language, but he grounds it in his own application and the rich tradition of the Cistercian contemplative. Through him, Trappist life becomes accessible, and contemplative prayer becomes attractive. He is an articulate poet who evokes our own hunger for more and affirms that desire for God is one that can be happily embraced no matter what era we are growing up within.

Transformation of the Human Person and Society

Merton is significant for contemporary spiritual seekers because he uses the language of hunger for issues pertaining to both contemplative prayer and social justice. He defies the separation between the activist and the person of prayer, inviting both to embrace a more integrated life and incorporate the contemplative dimension within the work for social transformation. His central concern is the transformation of the human person in intimate relationship with God. This transformation can reveal itself within the changing of unjust social structures. Thomas Merton gives us permission to wed these two desires within us and act upon them, to be both vocal advocate for social issues and deep contemplative within our own walls.

In Summary

Cistercian spirituality continues to influence many today through the writings of its great saints, religious leaders, and contemporary authors. Historically, other communities, such as the Bernardine Sisters, have adapted elements of the Cistercian charism into their own unique religious identity. Other religious communities have emerged as a response to the vitality found in the Cistercian charism. The monasteries of Cistercians, Trappists, and Trappistines throughout the world continue to be havens of silence and the ordered life amidst the frenetic movements of contemporary culture.

Whether through good literature offered by their writers through the centuries, retreats on their grounds, or a pause to pray the Liturgy of the Hours with them in their chapels, the communities of the Cistercian and Trappist family provide a reminder that another alternative is available to us. They serve as markers in the field of the call to a quieter lifestyle that can foster attentiveness to the holy. Through labor and love of God, they invite us to go deeper into the contemplative life and let all productivity and generosity of heart flow from there.

Questions for Reflection:

- Have you ever experienced a hunger for God that made you want to go off by yourself and just be with God? How have you fed that hunger in your life?
- Is there a place for silence in your life? How do you practice it?

Resources for Ongoing Study:

Bernard of Clairvaux. *On Loving God*. Cistercian Fathers Series 13. Washington, DC: Cistercian, 1974.
Butler, Cuthbert. *Western Mysticism*. New York: Harper & Row, 1966.
Merton, Thomas. *New Seeds of Contemplation*. New York: New Directions, 1972.
———. *The Seven Storey Mountain*. New York: Harcourt Brace, 1948.

Part I: Monastic Spirituality

William St. Thierry. *On Contemplating God. Prayer. Meditations.* From *The Works of William of St. Thierry*, Volume 1. Translated by Sister Penelope. Kalamazoo, MI: Cistercian, 1977.

PART II
Mendicant Spirituality

Introduction

THE MENDICANT SCHOOL OF spirituality emerged at a time in Christian history where the predominant form of spirituality was monasticism. As was mentioned in the first section of this book, monasticism's strength was its stable community life of prayer. However, in the Middle Ages this stability had become institutionalized into a rigid form that harbored abuses and restricted people's possibilities for holiness. A second umbrella category of mendicancy describes our next school of spirituality out of which many spokes of diversity grew.

The word "mendicant" comes from a Latin word "mendicans" meaning "to beg." It is a term used to characterize a beggar of alms. It is also a word referring to religious organizations that originally held no personal or communal property. Mendicant friars depended for their livelihood on the generosity of others, living mostly on alms.

In the twelfth century CE the needs of the times were great. Not unlike the present day, there were political conflicts that resulted in feudal wars between city-states and families. On a larger scale, religious conflict with Islam had escalated into a military defense of the Holy Roman Church and its desire to reacquire control of the Holy Land. This multicultural exposure to Near Eastern cultures through the incursions by the Crusades brought much bloodshed and much wealth. Many of these assaults on the Holy Land were camouflage for economic expansion and pillaging. Under a religious guise they became military conquests that would bring riches back from Jerusalem and create an entirely new economic class, the merchants.

Simultaneously with this emergence of a new class came the formation of new political entities. The development and rise of towns and

Part II: Mendicant Spirituality

cities as places of commerce challenged the existing feudal system. It was a struggle to maintain control over these developments, and the medieval papacy began to feel religious and political competition.

As the papacy rose to greater heights, it also faced the challenge of a new spiritual fervor, one that manifested in energetic and dedicated men and women who wanted to commit themselves wholeheartedly to the Gospel message but were exploring alternative approaches that deviated from the norms previously known in Christendom. Popes and bishops often did not know how to respond to this eruption of devotion and dedication that was being manifest in the youth of their day. They had to sort the authentic forms from the fraudulent ones, and which was which was not always clear. In addition, the challenges that these fledgling groups issued sometimes prompted some embarrassment and defensiveness from powerful prelates and potentates.

One such new grouping of zealous Christians was the mendicants. Through significant persons like St. Francis of Assisi, St. Clare, and St. Dominic, a new form of spiritual dedication reaffirmed radical dependence on God. Initially a lay movement, this form of spirituality welcomed people to live out their gospel call by stepping into the streets to preach and teach. Mendicants abandoned the surety and protection of monastic enclaves and formed communities that took on the Gospel challenge to rebuild the church, one that was aligned with the poor, the outcast, and the sick.

The mendicants preached in the villages, the cities, and the country, translating the teachings of Christ into simpler forms that uneducated laity could assimilate. Theirs was a popular spirituality, which ignited and spread throughout Western Europe like a wildfire. Radical in its inception, mendicants chose simplicity of life and mobility. They assembled into communities, but eschewed the comfort of buildings and property. Just as Jesus had nowhere to lay his head, they, too, began by wandering as itinerant preachers, receiving their sustenance directly from those who were moved by their witness or their need. Later, they lived in friaries, ministering to the disadvantaged and needy. These mendicants reached out beyond the established structures to catechize and educate populations that were largely unaddressed by the existing hierarchy.

The personalities of these early founders significantly affected the growth of this new form of spirituality. They were individuals with magnetism and charisma, marked by the Spirit and totally devoted to the

Introduction to Part II

church. They were not interested in breaking away in heretical fashion, but in bolstering up and reshaping the church among the people.

This spontaneous and charismatic movement erupted throughout Europe, growing at a phenomenal rate. Less easily controlled and confined than their counterparts in monasteries, the mendicants expressed their fidelity to Christ in the church and sought ratification of their efforts by Rome. Recognizing the authenticity in their inspiration, Pope Innocent III affirmed their growth and insisted on modified Rules for these young communities to ensure their longevity.

The organization of each mendicant school took its lead from the genius of their founders, responding to the signs of the times and the call of the Spirit. The formalization of these schools resulted in great diversity and division as the original fire of the founders was harnessed for subsequent generations.

In the following chapters we will look at three mendicant communities—the Franciscans, the Dominicans, and the Carmelites—and see how this extraordinary energy and passion manifested and congealed in new forms of religious life and spiritual fervor. Their witness and their vitality continue to draw people today to break through stale structures and open up the windows of the church and society to look again at the plight of the poor they serve.

4

Franciscan Spirituality
Mendicants as Friars Minores

THROUGHOUT HISTORY THERE ARE spiritual figures who signal an entirely new direction than has been known previously. Their lives speak across cultures and times and arrest the attention of idealistic people, as well as dedicated spiritual seekers. Such is the phenomenon we see in the persons of Saint Francis of Assisi and St. Clare, a man and a woman who continually inspire us over a thousand years after their birth. These two figures are two of the most electric and ecumenically attractive saints from history. Their ecological and emotional appeal makes them perennial witnesses to the need to honor God within the creation that explodes with divine glory.

The Milieu

In the introduction to Mendicant Spirituality, we have already seen how expansion and conflict marked the era in which the mendicant phenomenon occurred. The medieval milieu of the twelfth century CE had parallels to our own. There were significant historical developments as Christianity encountered other religious traditions such as Islam. Conflicts in the Middle East erupted as Christians tried to regain their control

Part II: Mendicant Spirituality

over sacred lands and Jerusalem. The Crusades were the attempts by the Holy Roman Empire to reacquire the Holy Land to which Christians and Jews could no longer travel safely. These campaigns unleashed major military assaults that affected all the lands en route from Rome to Jerusalem. Many atrocities were committed on both sides in an attempt to seize or maintain control.

The Crusades opened up new avenues for business ventures. Soldiers and ecclesial personnel saw opportunities in the newly acquired lands and exploited the possibilities for their homelands and households. As the wealth of the spoils of battle reached European soil, a new class of merchants emerged. These entrepreneurs needed laborers for the manufacture of cloth and other goods. The feudal system readily supplied them with poor landless workers who could be virtually enslaved in the production process.

Concern with the needs of these laborers was secondary to the flourishing of commerce. Issues of justice for the workers were not even considered worth the time of the newly affluent. The earliest roots of a capitalist system were forming, and competition between vendors further reduced any compassion that a merchant might have for his workforce.

The Founders

Now, picture the well-bred son of a wealthy businessman, the only child of a successful textile salesman who planned to follow his father into a lucrative career. His father is a Sunday churchgoer, who is a leading member of the local civic community. The son completes his studies and enjoys life with his buddies, an assortment of youth from other established business families in the city.

Like many youth in their prime, the son relishes his chances to prove his manhood. In the surrounding area there are numerous regional skirmishes, which could bode well or ill for his father's business undertakings. This young man is interested in promoting his family name and accomplishments. He enters into these battles with a certain naiveté and delight. In one conflict, he ends up wounded and returns home seriously ill.

This is the decisive moment.

The son has been changed in his battle experience.

Franciscan Spirituality

He is no longer interested in the success of his father's business, but after a lengthy convalescence turns his eye towards the disadvantaged and the downtrodden people who have suffered at the hands of a system that allows them little opportunity for breaking the cycle of poverty. He begins to attend to them and reach out to them in their suffering and identify with them.

His father is alarmed at this shift.

He attempts to shame his son in public into submission.

Instead, in the town square the son strips himself of his clothing, the fabric of his own father's story, and walks uninhibited out of the town into the fields where he begins to live out his original freedom.

It is 1204 CE. We are in Assisi, Italy. Our idealistic young adult is Francis of Assisi, eventually to be named a saint.

Next to him is Lady Clare, the daughter of the noble house of Offreduccio di Bernardino. In her youth, Clare only knew of Francis by reputation, since he was twelve years older. Eventually, she follows his lead into a life dedicated to prayer, contemplation, and rigorous spiritual discipline. Francis, her guide, gives her great freedom in the design of her own religious form of community life. Poverty is her focus, the incarnation of a life lived in total dependence on a generous Christ and the brothers of the order of St. Francis, but as women mendicants, the Poor Clares.

Francis and Clare bring a startling spiritual challenge to the feudal and monastic systems of the twelfth century. Their ascetical emphasis is an attempt to solve the problems of their era in a more active way than the spirituality of monasticism could. Franciscan spirituality is perhaps best known for its emphasis on simplicity, appreciation of nature, and the literal application of the Gospel by its founders. Both of these great figures continue to attract contemporary persons by their zeal, generosity, and radicalness. The Franciscan spiritual tradition includes men and women, lay and religious, throughout the world, who want to devote their lives to a complete spiritual dependence on God and the Gospel of Christ.

Spiritual Legacy for Today: A Fresh Inspiration

In any era a story such as Francis' strikes a chord: the idealistic child and the hardworking parent in a conflict. At different times in our lives we resonate with the various players in the drama. St. Francis of Assisi, one of

Part II: Mendicant Spirituality

the most revered and dramatic saints within the Christian tradition, still captivates us with his simplicity and daring challenges to contemporary comfort, complacency, and respectability.

The spiritual legacy of the Franciscans supports the call of all people, laity especially, to respond to the poor, to depend on God, and to renew the church. Therefore, we can say that the legacy it offers includes a broad, inclusive spirituality, radical dependence on God, a challenge to renew the church, a recultivation of missionary zeal and serving the poor, as well as the sentimental images of the Christmas crèche. We shall examine each of these now.

A Broad, Inclusive Spirituality

Initially a lay movement, Franciscan spirituality grew out of a hunger for greater authenticity and radical devotion. St. Francis was a layman who never asked for ordination. Instead, he continued to advocate for a broad spirituality, inclusive of *all* persons, whether wealthy or poor and uneducated. He identified with those estranged from the political or religious systems and excluded from the benefits of the culture. He saw Christ within the poor and brought that to the church's awareness. His affinity for the poor would propel slowly through history and lead to an articulated "option for the poor" in ecclesial circles in the twentieth century.

Complete Dependence on God

St. Francis adopted the mendicant spirituality of an open hand, of complete dependence on God and trust in the goodness of humanity. Francis took up the life of a wandering, itinerant preacher, speaking of penance and peace. He begged for his food and shelter, while offering freely the gift of his presence and his hopeful message about Christ. A gathering of followers joined him in his begging, and dedicated themselves to a radical rule of simplicity based strictly on the Gospel of Jesus Christ.

Renewal of the Church

In the place of their origin, Franciscans influenced the spread of renewal in the church of Europe. This was a direct response to the mandate

Franciscan Spirituality

Francis received early in the discernment of his call to "repair my church." Initially, he believed this message was confined to the renovation of the ruins of local churches, but later he grew to understand a broader call to attend to the disheveled aspects of the larger ecclesial body, and to offer an alternative to the stifling structures of the spirituality of his day. One of the most refreshing aspects of Franciscan spirituality was its organic, straightforward focus and simplicity, which got underneath the rubrics, regulations, and rituals to the essence of literal love of neighbor and God.

Missionary Zeal

With missionary energy building, Franciscans moved beyond Umbria in Italy to other areas of the globe. Francis attempted missionary expeditions to Spain, Morocco, and Egypt. This Good News to the marginalized and poor emanated out to all who were needy. This was a new phenomenon in Francis' time period. While Clare's charism called her into the cloister, Francis' impulse was to go beyond the conventional security of home and country to evangelize. "Preach the Gospel at all times," he is attributed with saying, "and when necessary use words."

Dedication to Serving the Poor

The Friars Minors by their very name, "minores," are dedicated to service to and with the poor. In their spirituality they identify with the poor of the world. Blind and seriously ill in the last years of his life, Francis incarnated the marginalized, impoverished, and suffering poor of the world. His devotion to the Eucharist and the crucified Christ was intense. Francis' identification with Christ revealed itself through the imprint of stigmata, wounds in his hands, feet, and side that replicated that of Christ.

The Christmas Crèche

Sensitive to what touched the lives of the simple people with whom he associated, Francis popularized the birth of Christ by bringing the nativity crèche into prominence. His affinity for the common person generated great affection for him by the needy. This popular devotion continued to be a visible reminder of the humanity of Christ for subsequent generations.

Part II: Mendicant Spirituality

A tender and tactile tableau of the abject simplicity into which the Christ child was born, the Christmas crib became one of the most rudimentary means for educating children about the birth of Christ and reconnecting the faithful each year with the incarnation mystery.

Contemporary Spiritual and Pastoral Contributions

Franciscan spirituality remains one of the most vital forms of mendicant spirituality even to this day. While St. Clare's personal spirituality is less known, she lived the same family of values behind cloistered walls as a woman and governed her sisters with the same passion and devotion as Francis. Jointly, she and Francis left behind gifts for future generations that are characterized by radical Gospel simplicity, ecological reverence, and hospitality.

Radical Gospel Simplicity

A radical Gospel simplicity grounds the powerful contribution of Franciscan spirituality for today's believers. Simplicity of life is a challenge for any era, but Franciscan spirituality invites us to examine the glut of goods that clutter our lives and reduce this complexity to simpler proportions. Clutter is a burden. It clogs up our freedom and prohibits us from a free and appreciative movement with the natural beauty of life and the hidden gifts of God. Restricting our possessions to items of need versus those of greed is a fundamental invitation in Franciscan spirituality.

Francis' call to listen to the Spirit and respond wholeheartedly defied the human propensity to complicate things through formalization and structure, too. His desire to allow his community to follow the simple rule of the Gospel in its literal understanding was judged insufficient by church hierarchy for years before the Rule for the Friars was accepted. Yet, gradually the wisdom and sanctity of his life moved the resistance, and new congregations were founded.

Many religious communities and secular orders take their inspiration from the Franciscan charism. In addition to the Friars Minor, there are Capuchins, missionary congregations like the Franciscan Missionaries of Mary, and Third Order groups. The Poor Clares continue to live the radical contemplative call to simplicity as women religious under the Rule of St. Clare.

Ecological Reverence

Intimate relationship with Creation is a hallmark of Franciscan spirituality. Proclaimed by Pope John Paul II as the Patron of Ecology in 1980, Francis epitomizes a radical sense of relationship with creation. Profoundly reverential towards the Creator, Francis knew that "right relationship" with God leads to "right relationship" with all that the Creator had given. That awareness changes the way we touch our world. It cannot be callous or harsh; it cannot be wasteful or extravagant. Francis of Assisi's reverence demands a brotherly affection and concern.

One of his most beautiful spiritual writings is the "Canticle of Brother Sun." Few historical figures have taken up such an intimate and positive approach to the material world. Paradoxically, Francis experimented with radical fasts and impositions on his flesh until he realized late in life that his body, "Brother Ass," deserved greater respect and acceptance. Today, Franciscans celebrate the reverential wisdom of their founder in works that uplift the body and celebrate nature. In a world habitually driven by material expectation, success, and environmental abuse, Franciscan spirituality reminds us of another way of relationship in reverence and delight. This spirituality celebrates simple obedience to the Holy Spirit and the joy of being a part of a larger creation.

Hospitality

Hospitality is highly valued in Franciscan spirituality. As mendicants, Franciscans have known throughout the centuries the great grace of being welcomed into the homes of others and fed by their generosity. They have been the recipients of others' hospitality. Therefore, Franciscan houses throughout the world emphasize welcoming visitors and strangers as a continuation of the practical application of charity that Francis espoused. This hospitality involves a sharing of resources, availability, accessibility, and a willingness to embrace all people, even "the lepers" in our lives, just as Francis embraced the lepers of his day.

Part II: Mendicant Spirituality

In Summary

The popularity of St. Francis and St. Clare outside their specific communities is still a testimony to their universality and timeliness. Many non-Christians, including Buddhists, Hindus, Native Americans, and even agnostics regard St. Francis as a saint close to their own tradition. Francis and Clare appeal to our youthful idealism and our fire for God. When we are with them in Spirit, we want to do more for God and give our all. This is a perennial inspiration that continues to serve the Spirit for generations after the Poor Man of Assisi and his faithful friend, Lady Clare, first responded generously to God's call.

Questions for Reflection:

- Have you ever seen any of that youthful idealism of Francis in your own life?
- Do you think you live a simple life? What are the indicators of this?

Resources for Ongoing Study:

Armstrong, Regis J., and Ignatius C. Brady, translators. *Francis and Clare.* New York: Paulist, 1982.
Boff, Leonardo. *St. Francis: A Model for Human Liberation.* Translated by J. Diercksmeier. New York: Crossroad, 1982.
Cronin, Kevin M., editor. *A Friar's Joy.* New York: Continuum, 1997.

5

Dominican Spirituality
Friars Preachers of the Truth

WHEN WE BEGIN TO inquire about Dominican spirituality, words like truth, preaching, and study are among those most frequently associated with the Order of Preachers. Indeed, no religious body prior to 1200 had dedicated itself to these three passions in the same way as the Friars Preachers did under the lead of their founder, St. Dominic. These pursuits were essential facets in their religious devotion and discipline. The rigor to which they gave themselves was a necessary response to the needs of the day within church history. Let us examine the milieu from which St. Dominic came forth and the spiritual motivation of this remarkable founder.

The Milieu

An era fraught with political aggression, heretical thought, and shrewd organization, the late twelfth century was a time of grave danger for the papacy and orthodox doctrine. Within the larger horizon of medieval Europe, ambitious Germanic princes threatened the stability and authority of the pope for over fifty years. Invading emperors, attempting to overtake

Rome and assert control over ecclesial properties and appointments, finally provoked Pope Innocent III to resort to armed defense.

Exacerbating the conflict, within the church itself there was pervasive criticism of corruption and materialism within the hierarchy. This disaffection prompted a revival of Manicheanism, a heresy dating from the time of St. Augustine, in a new form by the Albigensians. The Albigensians were an anti-Christian element that, in their struggle to explain the origin of evil, assumed a hostile stance towards matter, the body, marriage, and fruitful intercourse. From their perspective, earth and material reality were dark forces, which should be shunned. In southern France, they had organized churches, bishops, and liturgical life according to their viewpoint. Wealthy patrons supported the heretical doctrine, financing schools and workshops to promote the heretical perspective.

Pope Innocent III attempted to address the ignorance behind the heresy through persuasion and preaching. The way they were done, none of these attempts worked well. He sent Cistercian missionaries as official church emissaries to preach orthodox principles and correct the errors in theology. These were viciously murdered. There arose, then, a need for a new approach to the defense of religion and civilization, a re-instruction of the faith. To that end, a young Spanish canon-regular was called.

The Founder

Dominic Guzman (1170–1221 CE), just over thirty-five years of age, came into contact with the Cistercian mission to the Albigensians around 1206 in southern France after the killing of a papal legate while enroute to Denmark. He had been living as a friar under the rule of St. Augustine and had been appointed prior after only seven years of contemplative life.

Accompanied in his initial visit by an army led by Count Simon IV of Montfort, he realized the official pomp of the arriving delegates did nothing to help their case. He and his bishop, whom he was accompanying, suggested that an example of poverty might do more good than a display of clerical ceremony and power. His encounter with the Albigensians convinced Dominic that conversion of lapsed Christians could best be done through reasonable preaching and ascetical simplicity, not warlike force. Even though his preaching did not affect immediate change, he was convinced a peaceful approach with proper scholarship could effectively be morally persuasive. Supported by the Pope, Dominic began to preach and signed his name from this date on as "Brother Dominic, Preacher." Preaching previously was a right reserved only to bishops. Here was a shift in evangelization and policy with ecclesiastical authorities.

Dominic founded the Order of Preachers in 1214 CE to address through learning, scholarship, and preaching the need for conversion among the estranged Christians and non-Christians. His spirituality was a blend of traditions, which became distinctive as a whole, valuing the recitation of the Office, study, penance, preaching, communal life, and contemplation. He produced few writings in his lifetime with the exception of a few letters. His legacy to his followers was not a rule or a body of literature but a profound conviction to the apostolate of preaching. Dominic died of an illness at age fifty-two, having founded sixty friaries in eight provinces, extending from Poland, Scandinavia, and Palestine, to England, France, and Italy.

Spiritual Legacy for Today: Truth and Study

The extent of religious and catechetical ignorance in Dominic's day was vast. There was no vehicle to correct or guide common persons in their understanding of God. Many were victims of charismatic speakers who led them away from healthy spiritual principles. Dominic was focused on correctives for this reality in his own day and he encouraged educated understandings through the Dominican religious community. Therefore, the spiritual legacy he left behind incorporated his dedication to the promotion of salvation for all, an emphasis on the pursuit of truth, and the necessity of study as aids to healthy spiritual thought.

The Salvation of All

Dominic's profound concern was the salvation of others, rather than personal sanctification. This was a new approach historically, for most spiritual communities had gathered together and been formed around the purpose of personal holiness. Their emphasis was on saving their own souls through the rule of the founder. Dominic's emphasis was instead placed on the results of the apostolate itself, loving their neighbor with a care and concern for their conversion to truth. Holiness of life was still valued, but his attention was less with his own spiritual progress and more with the needs of his neighbor. His dedication to the educational and moral uplifting of persons, who were confused by heretical teaching and thought, produced a new spirituality.

The Pursuit of Truth

Pursuit of truth underscored Dominican spirituality. But this pursuit was always a truth that was a "who" rather than a "what." Knowledge begot love according to the wisdom of the great Dominican theologian, St. Thomas Aquinas. Within the spiritual realm, it was this love which was the central purpose of Christian spirituality. The Dominican style of living this love has manifested itself in persons whose lives were filled with activity, scholarship, and contemplation, all in the interest of contributing to the good of their neighbor. Dominican spirituality melded knowledge and love in an undivided whole.

The Necessity of Study

To safeguard the proper preparation of Dominican friars and nuns for this work, there was a necessity to study with scholars at the most orthodox and solid universities in Europe. An obligation to study produced an order of professional theologians, many of whom are significant historical heavyweights in the Christian tradition. We have the Dominicans to thank for the brilliant insights of three Doctors of the Church: St. Albert the Great (ca. 1200–1280), St. Thomas Aquinas (ca. 1225–1274), and St. Catherine of Siena (1347–1380). We also have mystics such as Meister Eckhart (ca. 1260–1328), who were nourished within the Dominican family. This emphasis in the Dominican school of spirituality promoted reason and scholarship as means to solid faith formation. Methodical attention to thorough study is a primary element of Dominic's legacy.

Contemporary Spiritual and Pastoral Contributions

In recent decades there has been a reaction against the intellectual aspects of the spiritual life. Perhaps this is the repercussion of many centuries of reinforcement of excessively rational defenses of faith and theology. In eras where many contradictory theories and philosophies abounded, the likelihood of intellectually weak and imbalanced ideas was strong. Dominican spirituality challenges us to think things through from the basis of the primal commandments of Jesus Christ: love of God and love of neighbor. This involves using all of our faculties to help us go deeper. The spiritual and pastoral contributions of the Dominican school of spirituality include, therefore, the value of the intellect in the spiritual life, new religious structures, and a vast array of theological and spiritual writings from which we can educate ourselves and be stretched.

The Value of the Intellect in the Spiritual Life

Our age is one of pluralism and religious dialogue that has opened up conversations never previously held. This openness is desirable, but without careful scholarship and thorough reflection we are vulnerable to misunderstanding, misinterpretation, and mediocrity. A major contribution that the Dominican tradition gives to contemporary persons is the reminder that the intellect has a role to play in a grounded spiritual life. The emotional dimension in the spiritual life is valuable, as is the physical and relational. But the Dominican tradition reinforces the necessity of a continual integration of the mind through study and reflection.

Prayer is enhanced, as well, through this integration. The resources left behind by great masters encourage a prayer life that is complemented by study and reflection. A valuable gift from this school of spirituality is ongoing intellectual writing and research that can inform our spiritual questioning.

A New Religious Structure

The Dominicans or Friars Preachers were the first religious order founded as an organized army of priests around a Master General and arranged into provinces. Prior to their foundation, priests and monks were affiliated with specific monastic houses and bound specifically to them. The Friars Preachers revised the monastic structure and the traditional stability associated with vows to one monastery. They established a new form of governance under the direction of a central superior. This superior could assign the friars wherever they were needed.

Part II: Mendicant Spirituality

The Friars Preachers' allegiance was broad. It extended beyond autonomous houses and individual leadership to a broader region and enterprise. This was an innovation not seen prior to the 1200s and it has served as a model for every religious order since. Conformity was not the main focus. Dominic believed in the community and he held the conviction that the group had greater insight than any single person. This conviction is seen in the structures he established for the rule. The principal concern was always how to be helpful and useful to the souls of their neighbors. The larger body of friars often had greater insight into the needs of others than a single, presiding superior could have. The confreres devoted themselves to identifying the needs and moving to the places where those needs could be addressed as a part of the Dominican community.

Theological and Spiritual Writings

The cumulative body of literature gathered from the great Dominican writers is a significant treasure for contemporary spiritual and pastoral use. The Dominican tradition has spawned a wealth of resources for persons with questions about theological thought and spiritual enrichment.

Thomas Aquinas' tome in the *Summa Theologiae* is a valuable scholastic tool for any theological study. Much of Western theological thought finds its base in Thomistic theology. Catherine of Siena's wisdom in guiding popes through schismatic difficulties is founded in a rich mystical life which began for her around age seven. Her book of *The Dialogue* is a powerful spiritual manual. Meister Eckhart, another great Dominican mystic, wrote extensively about the apophatic aspects of the spiritual life, using his own experience as a means to explain this nebulous strain of mystical awareness. These are just three of many Dominican writers who contribute to the spiritual insights amassed within Christianity.

In Summary

Dominican spirituality adapted the strengths of conventual life seen in monasteries and religious houses of its day with apostolic outreach that took them beyond the confinements of their specific regions. The constitution of the Order is borrowed from the customs of other communities of Dominic's time, Augustinian, Premontre, and Cistercian monasticism.

Dominican Spirituality

But the attitude toward communal life was secondary to the central value of study and preaching. Dominic's vision was that all elements of study, common life, prayer, and liturgy would blend harmoniously in the service of preaching. Love of God and love of neighbor were the two aspects of Dominican spirituality that flowed from one another.

Questions for Reflection:

- Is your spirituality nurtured more by your intellect or your heart?
- What literature has fed your spiritual development?

Resources for Ongoing Study:

Catherine of Siena. *The Dialogue.* Translated by S. Noffke. Classics of Western Spirituality. New York: Paulist, 1980.

Thomas Aquinas. *Summa Theologiae.* Edited by Thomas Gilby. Garden City, NY: Image, 1969.

Tugwell, Simon, editor. *Early Dominicans: Selected Writings.* Classics of Western Spirituality Series. New York: Paulist, 1982.

6

Carmelite Spirituality
A Mendicant and Mystical Style

THE TERM "CARMELITE" FOR many faithful Catholics is not an entirely foreign name. The genius and writings of great Spanish mystics like St. Teresa of Avila and the poetry of St. John of the Cross, as well as the simple way of St. Therese of Lisieux, have made many of us aware of the Carmelite tradition. In the twentieth century, Elizabeth of the Trinity and Edith Stein chose to follow in the footsteps of "hermits" who lived the mendicant life, beggars within a contemplative community of Carmel.

Many of us, however, may know little about the spirituality of Carmel that inspired such great men and women within the Catholic Christian tradition. A radical life of prayer, focused on knowing the love of God through contemplation, may appear to be irrelevant for contemporary Christians "in the world." Yet, we are drawn to look again to see what riches lie within this ancient tradition, a mendicant lifestyle within monastic structures and rhythms of life.

The Milieu

The time is the earliest days of the 1200s, after Richard the Lionhearted in the Crusades of 1191 reclaimed from Moslem control the narrow stretch of land from which juts up Mount Carmel. Situated on the northern coast of Palestine in the Holy Land, Mount Carmel held great significance in the history of Judaism. It was a place where prophets encountered Yahweh. Cooled by the breezes from the Mediterranean, this site was incredibly appealing for reflection and prayer.

The Founders

Historical documentation dates the organized movement at Mount Carmel to the thirteenth century, yet the spirit of the tradition stems all the way back to the earliest days of the Jewish prophets, Elijah and Elisha. Radical and prophetic figures, these men spent much of their lives near Mount Carmel. The first hermits of the Carmelite tradition began living on Mount Carmel near a spring identified as "the fountain of Elijah."

No records were kept by the earliest Carmelites. Pilgrims on their way to Jerusalem spotted them in the early 1200s. The oldest documentation that exists is in the form of the *Rubrica Prima*, which identified the members of the order as endorsed by Pope Honorius, who succeeded Pope Innocent III (the Pope who officially acknowledged the Franciscan community). Primarily composed of devout men, these first Carmelites reordered their values and converted to a serious lifestyle in the spirit of their liege and Lord, Jesus Christ. They committed themselves as pilgrims to the only reality that would fill their restlessness and longing for God.

Under the guidance of Albert, the patriarch of Jerusalem, these lay penitents began lives of solitude, silence, and ongoing prayer in attempts to follow Jesus as hermits. When possible, daily Eucharist was celebrated in a common chapel. Asceticism was essential in their lives. Later, a mandate of poverty was imposed on them by Pope Gregory IX.

By 1238 the political climate of the region deteriorated between the Moslems and the Christians, and the hermits emigrated to Cyprus, Sicily, England, and France. They adapted their lifestyle as hermits to the religious climate of Western Europe and, with papal approval, took on a mendicant form, following in the footsteps of the Dominican and Franciscan friars. They began living in dormitories, preaching, studying, and administering the sacraments. Their monastic stability changed to mendicant mobility with a commitment to pastoral ministry in urban

Part II: Mendicant Spirituality

contexts. In 1452 Rome approved the admittance of women to a second order of Carmelites.

Many religious communities attempted to reform themselves in the Middle Ages. A major historical shift within the Carmelites occurred in the fifteenth and sixteenth centuries. In an attempt to recover the essence of the early eremitic tradition, Teresa of Avila and John of the Cross continued reform efforts that had begun the century before by Blessed John Soreth. The result of these reforms was the evolution in 1593 of the Discalced Carmelites (OCD) (discalced referring to their lack of shoes). This reform marked a return to deliberate, healthy community life, composed of moderate asceticism and an emphasis on prayer. The Carmelite Friars (OCarm) continued in their own development as an autonomous community, honoring the original call to Carmel by instituting reform in the seventeenth century regarding prayer.

Central to the spirituality of Carmel was a strong devotion to Mary, the Mother of Jesus, and an identification with Elijah, the prophet. This devotion to Mary is evidenced throughout the world in the naming of cloisters after Our Lady of Carmel. Since the seventeenth century she has continued to be a central figure within the spirituality of Carmel.

Spiritual Legacy for Today: Contemplation and Unitive Love

The tradition of Carmel has an amazing number of devout mystics who sought to love God and neighbor through a mysticism of love. Union with God—a single-minded, simple, focused attentiveness—was valued and promoted in the community, especially following the reforms. This straightforward approach shaped the passion and seriousness that defines the spirituality of the Carmelite community in monastic settings. We will examine this legacy of single-mindedness, solitude and community, and the wearing of the brown scapular here.

Single-mindedness

Single-mindedness characterized the heart of the Carmelite instruction on prayer. Union with God in love required a wholehearted surrender of one's self to that relationship. Nothing but God could fill the many holes inside of a person. No religion, no doctrine, no spiritual movement or ministry could fulfill the primordial hunger for more. Only God could meet the soul on that level. John of the Cross proclaimed that "nada, nada, nada" (nothing, nothing, nothing) could replace or substitute for God.

Such a single-minded fascination with God was absolutely necessary, especially in the inevitable valleys of the spiritual journey. In the darkness that resulted, only a deep commitment to the God of love helped the seeker survive the weaning from attachments that interfered with total dependence on God. Seeking God through these nights, even though they challenged all the assumptions of the seeker, ultimately led to higher planes of intimacy and freedom with God according to John of the Cross.

This single-minded devotion to God had an effect on the very makeup of the human being who gave herself or himself to it. John's own relationship with God brought about his radical personality transformation, converting his somewhat abrasive style of being into one that was richly compassionate and charitable. Spiritual union carried serious consequences when taken up deliberately.

Solitude and Community

The spirituality of the Carmelites also issued its members an invitation to formatively blend both solitude and community. The earliest Carmelites lived very solitary lives in the desert, which taught them things that no other landscape could have. When they moved out of Carmel onto European soil, their call to desert solitude had to adapt to an interior form, although their understanding of themselves as hermits living in community continued unchanged.

Community had always been valued in their Rule, but now it became more obviously necessary. "Communal life" now manifested in such activities as regular prayer with the Psalms, shared meals, and ministry that reached out to a broader world. While the writings of the community stressed the eremitical (hermit) origins of prayer and solitude as a mainstay, their actual lifestyle reflected a strong communal practice, which sustained their ministry and their charity.

Part II: Mendicant Spirituality

The Brown Scapular

One notable spiritual practice and devotion, the wearing of the brown scapular, was promoted by the Carmelite community. Historically, representing the yoke of obedience to God and later a sign of dedication, the Carmelites wore a scapular as a part of their identification with their Order. This practice was transmitted to a broader population in the nineteenth and early twentieth century: a small brown felt neckband with the image of Mary stitched onto it was worn under the garment of the devotee. It served as a constant reminder of reliance on Mary's promise that salvation would be granted to those who willingly submitted to God's plan.

Contemporary Spiritual and Pastoral Contributions

With such a sober focus, it may be thought that Carmelite spirituality is a cheerless one with little to offer contemporary seekers. Such is not the case. The Carmelite tradition has produced an abundance of spiritual resources that include poetry and mystical metaphors to illustrate the process of growth in the spiritual life. Additionally, their writings have exposed the human tendency towards self-deception and illusion as an escape in the spiritual life. Their extensive reflection on their prayer experiences have provided fabulous resources for deepening the life of prayer for those who hunger to do so. Let us examine each of these contributions.

Poetry

A harsh and functional world like ours needs poetry. Perhaps, one of the greatest contributions of the Carmelite legacy that personally touches contemplative seekers and literary buffs alike is the poetry of St. John of the Cross. In a world starved of spiritual beauty and intimacy, the literary genius of St. John is rich fare. His writings consist of four commentaries on mystical poetry, solicited by those who sought spiritual direction from him. In these he outlines the spiritual journey in the relational and colorful tradition of Song of Songs from the Hebrew Scriptures. In recent times, his poetic creativity has been acknowledged as some of the finest literature of all time. The passionate language and imagery has the capability of renewing our souls in each reading. His poetry is an excellent starting place to get acquainted with his works.

Mystical Metaphors

If imagery is a central aspect of Generation-X spirituality, Teresa of Avila could appeal to modern seekers in her rich language of metaphor. Her analogy of the spiritual life as the watering of a garden, using different means of cultivation, instructs and stretches the reader. Her language is that of her day and, therefore, the reader must be flexible in extending courtesy regarding the historical limitations of her constructs. But her mystical metaphors speak of mansions and silkworms, the pastoral images from the fields and cities of her day, still evoking the creative mind and inviting the contemplative soul to journey deeper into relationship with God.

She also wrote lengthy letters to her religious sisters to guide them on their path. The tone in these letters is chatty but solid. There is a warmth and ease in her style that is attractive and amusing. Her vignettes and examples carry humor and charm.

Her autobiography is also a wonderful book that exposes us to her human vulnerabilities. A candid disclosure of her own falls along the spiritual path, this writing is candid and humble, beguiling in its self-assessment and unmasking of her own illusions. Her modeling and her instruction continue to provide valid guidance and wisdom for the spiritual seeker today.

Self-Awareness with No Illusion

A major contribution that Carmelite contemplatives offer the contemporary spiritual seeker is a no-nonsense pragmatism about human nature. Desert spirituality, out of which the Carmelites came, endorses a radical honesty about the human mix of blindness and beauty within. Similar to Zen Buddhism, this candor about the human propensity for self-deception is strongly articulated in the writings of Saints Teresa of Avila and John of the Cross. Concrete assistance for willingly giving up the protective devices we use to shield ourselves from our own limitedness is offered by both of these saints. Their works are correctives, inviting us to not fear to look at our own humanness; God's love is broad and deep enough to cushion us in our humility.

Prayer

Most of us associate the tradition of Carmel with prayer. This tradition brings us back to the essentials of the spiritual life. The Carmelite community, an unflinching advocate for prayer, continuously reminds us that this is a non-negotiable. In order to deepen spiritually, there is no substitute for prayer. Habitual prayer fosters maturity in the spiritual path. It engenders transparency and honesty with God and with self. Prayer, thoughtfully practiced, renews freedom and keeps us flexible in the hand of God. The need to declare false selves and false gods that interfere with the genuine emergence of the true self is perennial. No matter what era we are in, the Carmelites give a clarion call to return to God fully without reservation.

A mystical orientation is markedly apparent within the individuals and the spiritual legacy transmitted through the ages within the Order of Carmel. Honesty with ourselves leads us to greater honesty with God. For the Carmelite, that true self is the means to holiness, a prize worth gold to spiritual seekers of all times. Carmelite mysticism is a mysticism grounded in desert wisdom. Gutsy, stalwart, and bare bones in its quality, the mysticism of Carmel offers a counterpoint to the flowery, emotive mysticism of English and German mystics. It is sometimes spare in its style, but always turns us back to prayer and intimacy with God.

In Summary

Contemplative life and the constant attentiveness to prayer are significant elements in the Carmelite tradition. A focus on God alone characterizes the writings of the many great Carmelites. In poetry and prose, these writers contribute greatly to the mystical literature within the contemplative tradition. The Carmelites of today remind us that at the center of every Christian life should be the person of Christ without hesitation or compromise. This conviction challenges contemporary people to remember the essence of Christian spiritual life and choose it, if we dare.

Questions for Reflection:

- Does silence attract you? Are you comfortable with it?
- Have you ever used poetry for your prayer?

Resources for Ongoing Study:

Kavanaugh, Kieran, and Otilio Rodriguez, translators. *The Collected Words of St. John of the Cross*. Washington, DC: ICS, 1991.

Kavanaugh, Kieran, and Otilio Rodriguez, translators. *The Collected Works of St. Teresa of Avila*. 3 vols. Washington, DC: ICS, 1976–1985.

Paul-Marie of the Cross. *Carmelite Spirituality in the Teresian Tradition*. Translated by Kathryn Sullivan. Washington, DC: ICS, 1997.

Welch, John. *The Carmelite Way: An Ancient Path for Today's Pilgrim*. Mahwah, NJ: Paulist, 1996.

PART III

Ministerial and Active Apostolic Spirituality

Introduction

MINISTERIAL OR ACTIVE APOSTOLIC spirituality had a two-pronged focus in its inception: respond to the educational and spiritual needs of people whose illiteracy affected their spiritual development, and acknowledge the physical and social needs of those served. This form of spirituality was a combination of an internal call to dedicate one's life to God, manifested through external expressions of that conversion by improving the conditions in the world and spreading the Christian message. This third school of spirituality emerged out of a need to catechize the ignorant and recognize the social deprivations at the same time.

Active ministerial spirituality was evident in Christianity in its earliest days. The example of instruction and active attentiveness to the needs of the people was best seen in the human figure of Jesus Christ himself. He was not only interested in feeding people's spiritual lives, but also in nourishing them in other ways. His ministering to the widows who approached him, the women impoverished by the social system, and the poor and victimized was depicted throughout all four Gospel accounts. Luke's text particularly highlighted Jesus' championing of those abandoned or abused by the structures of the day.

The early Apostles picked up the modeling in their own apostolic activity. Concern with the spiritual lives of those to whom they preached was matched by concern for their physical and emotional needs. Cures by the disciples in the Acts of the Apostles continued to witness to an active engagement with the blind, the lame, and the hungry in the street. Early in the foundation of Christianity, the apostles recognized the need for active ministry in the equitable distribution of goods to widows and orphans among them. To attend to both the spiritual and material needs

Part III: Ministerial and Active Apostolic Spirituality

of those dependent on their charity and generosity, they ordained men as deacons and designated faithful women to care for those in hardship.

Christian spirituality was, therefore, a spirituality that practiced open and active ministerial involvement. So important was this balance among the original community that, when hardship fell on the Jerusalem Christians with the destruction of the Temple in 70 CE, the leadership of the Christian communities throughout the Roman Empire displayed their awareness of social responsibility by generating support for those most affected in the Holy Land. Goods and financial support were readily offered along with emotional and spiritual care.

Historically, however, with the development of monastic spirituality in the fourth century and its emphasis on removal from the commercial life of the cities, the active apostolic dimension of Christian spirituality seemed to go underground in many ways. The view for centuries was that the spiritual life could best be developed in a place separate from common lay life. Monastics brought their aspirants to a place where community was emphasized and the rhythm of prayer was shaped around a daily fixed schedule. The only opportunity for religious education for generations was inside the walls of the monasteries or among the religious elite. Holiness was thought to be best achieved by extracting one's self from the workaday world and devoting one's life to prayer and ascetical practice.

While the ministry done in monasteries cannot be discounted, monastics were confined to their compounds. The needy had to come to the monk to be educated in the faith or relieved of their plight. This excluded the majority of the population.

Certainly, this was a valid option for persons inclined towards a monastic lifestyle, but what ministerial schools of spirituality did was open up the gates of education and spiritual life to those outside the walls of the enclosure. This movement challenged the assumption that holiness of life could best be attained through escape or enclosure from the world and renewed the vocational call to service as a valid and valuable response to the Spirit's call to spiritual devotion.

In the sixteenth and seventeenth centuries, this reclamation of the active ministerial approach to spirituality was a response to the signs of the times when serious religious ignorance marked much of the European continent. The church wanted to address the crippling illiteracy which led people into heretical ways of thinking. An important contribution of active ministerial religious communities was their investment of personnel and energy in responding to this vacuum in education, knowledge, and ministration.

Active ministerial spirituality allowed for diverse responses to the call of the spiritual life. Evangelization and pastoral work were reclaimed as vocational options for those dedicated to God. With the evolution of active apostolic spirituality, inspired and concerned men and women began to explore other approaches to meet these needs. Forms of prayer conducive for active ministry brought prayer out from behind the grille and the structured life into a way of living that saw God as housed within the activity of life. A new breadth of vision encouraged the individual and the communities of religious called to active life to find God within the realities of labors in the secular world.

Concern with the social welfare of the masses also grew in subsequent centuries. This movement of the Spirit took the ministers into the homes, schools, businesses, and churches where the masses lived and addressed that need right there in that milieu. They went into the work world of the poor and tried to confront the ignorance and illnesses they met there. Eventually, they built schools, hospitals, and social centers to concretely meet the educational, medical, and communal needs of those who lacked these services.

For over five hundred years these schools of spirituality have confirmed that depth in the spiritual life is not restricted to the monk, the beggar, and the hermit. Active ministerial spirituality recognized the face of the hidden Christ in the person on the street and actively chose to meet that figure through direct acts of compassion, care, and concern. Religious communities of active women and men, ordained and lay, provided a new model for spiritual vitality. Social structures that ignored justice or neglected the health of the worker were challenged. The emergence of the professional minister who addressed the social needs of the time was the result of this active apostolic phenomenon. Conversion of the individual was matched in its importance by conversion of communities and structures. This school of spirituality raised awareness that conversion of institutions towards humane and just practices was an important and desirable sign of the conversion of society.

Vocationally, the active ministerial style of spirituality has had great generativity beyond the boundaries of the religious communities who practice this form of life, too. In recent times the emergence of lay ecclesial ministers has been the result of the active ministerial spiritual thrust.

Part III: Ministerial and Active Apostolic Spirituality

As a spirituality situated in the heart of human activity, active apostolic involvement occurs in the marketplace, where as a community of faith all can witness to the need for conversion. This school of spirituality acknowledges and affirms the foundational baptismal call of all people to evangelize and shape the world. Laity have been raised up to respond in kind to this call to education and service. They have been encouraged to extend the practice of what they saw modeled by all those active ministers whose spiritual lives and vocations took them right into the center of human need.

With such a breadth of possibilities for service, this third umbrella category of apostolic service has spawned exceptionally diverse groups who fit underneath its roof. The number of active ministerial congregations exploded throughout the last five hundred years, many of whom developed missionary dimensions to domestic and foreign countries. In Part III we will now look at four forms of spirituality from communities whose calling took them into apostolic ministry: Ignatian spirituality, Redemptorist or Alphonsian spirituality, Salesian spirituality, and Marist spirituality.

7

Ignatian Spirituality
Spirituality in a World of Action

WHEN WE LOOK AT the significant figures who have dramatically shaped contemporary spirituality, undoubtedly we must name Ignatius of Loyola as a major contributor. His vision, his flexibility, and his awareness of the needs of people in his day took him into the schools, the streets, and the spiritual life to explore radically new ways to lead people to Christ. In this chapter we look at his story.

The Milieu

The time was 1521 CE.

On the European continent, a reform was brewing. Western Christendom was in crisis. The Protestant Reformers had criticized the abuses in the papacy, challenged the spiritual laxity among many clerics and the hierarchy, and unmasked the economic rationale for many burdensome "spiritual" mandates. Rome was struggling in its response to this rebellion. The Inquisition was established but limped with its responsibilities and self-righteousness. Western Christendom was fractured, confused, and afraid. There was a need for strong leadership and a new form of spirituality that renewed the church and could bring individuals back into an ordered relationship with God.

The Founder

In Pamplona, Spain, a thirty-year-old Basque soldier was severely wounded in the leg while defending a fortress against French forces. He was fierce in his commitment to his home and schooled in the courtly manners of his noble family. During his convalescence, he read the only literature available that his sister-in-law could provide, the lives of the saints. While he longed for swashbuckling novels of knightly valor, he could not help but notice the courage, bravery, and radicality in the lives about those he was reading. He began to reflect on his life.

A profound spiritual transformation ignited within him. His identity as a worldly courtier and knight in pursuit of worldly ideals slowly shifted. He was moved by prayer and ascetical discipline to reform himself into a "knight" dedicated to the service of the Trinity. A religious vocation began to develop.

St. Ignatius of Loyola (1491–1556) was a mystic, an activist, a priest, and founder of the Society of Jesus, known as the Jesuits. His writings, inspired partially by his reading of the Rule of St. Benedict, are the result of Ignatius' direct experience of the Trinity, an encounter that propelled him into a radical new approach to the spiritual life and the needs of his time.

The outpouring of his zeal was manifest in the founding of colleges, universities, charitable institutions, and pastoral activity. From his "Company" began a new ministerial approach that was active and engaged with the cultural realities of the day. It also promoted a missionary outreach that spread beyond Europe into Asia. He engaged himself with religious zeal and a spiritual grounding in the needs of the church and the sociopolitical issues of his culture. He and his confreres actively addressed the confusion of the era, informed themselves theologically, and modeled fidelity and committed relationship with God and the church in a time when many abandoned both.

Today, Ignatius of Loyola's influence continues to renew us and challenge our complacency. Within retreat houses, renewal centers, and university classrooms, the call to spiritual authenticity and depth in relationship with God endures. As founder of the largest Catholic religious order, the Jesuits, Ignatius' distinctive style continues to challenge us and our contemporaries. It is a tradition that has had vast influence over the course of the last six hundred years.

Spiritual Legacy: A Unique Active Apostolic Spirituality

The unique contribution of Ignatian spirituality was its embeddedness in the world of action. Prior to the emergence of Ignatius' genius, spiritual schools that dominated the religious horizon were primarily monastic and mendicant in their forms. Each of these in their own way focused on a spiritual life that was structured through prayer, work, and study. Each of them had challenged the secure religious assumptions and limits of previous eras. Now, additional forms were needed.

The legacy that Ignatius left behind reflects this new awareness that God and the religious person can be embedded in the world and active in response to that world. It is out of that engagement that institutions and individuals can be transformed spiritually, pastorally, and culturally. The spiritual life is not one of remote withdrawal but presence in the world, where God can and does communicate with God's people and lead them. Discernment on how to respond to this revelation is a major task in the spiritual life. Let us look at this legacy of Ignatius of Loyola and his Jesuit companions.

Embeddedness in the World of Action

St. Ignatius challenged the complacency of those in the era in which he lived. Rather than retreating from the world into a spirituality of the day that isolated and insulated the person, Ignatius charged into the world, embracing a reverential love of creation and seeing all of it in service of God. God could be found in all things, and all things could be found in God. It was an active spirituality that valued the world and wanted to bring about its fulfillment in Christ.

Building on his own aptitude toward action, Ignatius reflected on how his natural propensity could be placed at the service of God. He began to see how God was revealing God's Self within the realities of an active life, that prayer itself could be melded into a life that took one beyond the confines of a chapel and made it manifest itself within the everyday rhythms of a life of work, study, play, and relationship. God was not restricted to set periods of time and specific practices and prayers, but was continually revealing God's Self in all forms of life. Ignatius himself modeled how to take notice of God infused in all aspects of life.

Transformation of Individuals and Institutions

Out of his radical service to the world emerged a dedication to the transformation of institutions and individuals. An active apostolic approach to ministry brought the Jesuits out into the streets to work as missionary evangelists, worker priests, academics, pastoral agents, and retreat directors. The Gospel of Jesus Christ became a motivating energy for changing social structures and bringing people into responsible empowerment. Ignatian spirituality was a call to action and acknowledgement that the Gospel was a countercultural and nonviolent revolution.

In tandem with this call to action was a call to justice. Transformation required an evaluation of injustice within the systems of society. Such a focus demanded that changes be made when such assessments revealed unjust situations and attitudes. This element of Ignatian spirituality would find new expression with the support of the Second Vatican Council in the 1960s, when an emphasis would be placed on the conversion of the larger world by a church that was firmly planted within the culture and called to evangelize it.

A Spiritual Life of Direct Communication with God

Prayer served the development of this revolutionary attitude, ordering and shaping it by fostering an intimate relationship with and commitment to God. It required a constant reformation from within, in dialogue, evaluation, and honesty with one's self and God.

Ignatius had the audacity to claim in the exercises, which emerged from his own spiritual journey, that a person could actually seek and find the will of God that was specific to that person, and that God directly wanted to communicate with the soul. All religious experience and prayer were a means of ascertaining the will of God for them and reforming one's life accordingly. All spiritual endeavors were valued according to how they assisted the seeker in tempering the inordinate desires that blocked fulfillment in God.

This access to the will of God was not a hidden wisdom, exclusive to religious professionals either. It was available to all people of faith. God was communicating constantly with all people of good will. The key to discerning this will was to notice the movements and invitations of God and respond whole-heartedly to God's call.

The Use of Imagination and Reflection in Prayer

Ignatian spirituality promoted the use of imagination, reflection, emotions, and desire to reach and touch God. Unlike many schools of spirituality before, which discounted and even discouraged the imaginative capacities of the human person, Ignatius affirmed that God could be actively perceived within the movements, sentiments, and orientations of the human heart. All faculties of the mind, the heart, and the will, including one's memory, were to be put in service of God's plan.

Within the life of prayer, greater depth and insight could occur through systematic reflection on the experience of prayer. Ignatius encouraged extensive reflection and attentiveness to prayer as a means of clarifying the motivations beneath them. In this way the tendency towards self-deception and superficiality could be acknowledged and consciously addressed.

Discernment in the Spiritual Life

However, one had to hone one's awareness of what was being revealed within these movements and craft one's response according to the will of God. This involved discernment. Ignatius was a master of human psychology even before the advent of the scientific study of the psychological. He used his own life as a laboratory of experimentation to see what dynamics had contributed to his spiritual advancement or regression.

Ignatius spent years examining his own spiritual yearnings, inclinations, impulses, and desires. He reflected on his own trials and errors in moving into mystical experience. His intense reflection produced phenomenal insight that advanced knowledge of the interior struggles of the human person. These guidelines opened up new vistas for integration of all aspects of the human person into the spiritual life. This systematic and thorough process became the basis for a new methodology for discerning the roots and origins of movements within a person's inner life. It became a form of discernment for major life choices and decision-making in daily challenges.

Contemporary Spiritual and Pastoral Contributions

Of the many historical schools of spirituality that have survived to the present day, few have had as far-reaching an impact as that of Ignatian spirituality. Conceived and born in an era resembling our own, with schismatic movements, hierarchical criticism, institutional decline, and spiritual resurgence, Ignatian spirituality has survived the test of time and has flourished in its many forms and ministerial adaptations. An active spirituality that refuses to retreat from the world that calls to us for help, the Ignatian tradition continues to challenge us to remember that God is everywhere, and our response to God is our collaboration in personal and societal reform.

Most notable of the contributions that the Ignatian school of spirituality has given to modern Christians are structured methods for self-examination, spiritual discernment, and reform. St. Ignatius' legacy is a detailed series of exercises through which individual and communal conversion can occur.

St. Ignatius used the term "Spiritual Exercises" to encompass every method of examination of consciousness, meditation and contemplation, including verbal and mental prayer, which might lead the practitioner into greater awareness of God and compliance with God's will. The flexibility that Ignatius espoused in his teaching about the different exercises is pertinent for today, for all forms were meant to be adaptable to the specific person, intent on removing any disordered attachments from his or her life that distracted him or her from following God completely. In Ignatius' style of spirituality, all exercises should dispose us to freedom.

We will highlight three "exercises" that originate in the Ignatian tradition: Examen of Consciousness, a daily spiritual review; the directed eight day retreats, a weeklong spiritual encounter; and a thirty day spiritual retreat, a month of spiritual exercises.

Examen of Consciousness

Originally called "the Examination of Conscience," this practice is an exercise done twice daily. It is meant to increase the practitioner's awareness of how God is moving in them, and how they are responding in the concrete events of everyday life. Each examen requires fifteen to twenty minutes to turn the practitioner's mind to God, to acknowledge that presence, to invite God to review together half of the day and to reveal moments of collaboration with the Holy Spirit and moments of dissonance.

After revisiting the day's actions, an intentional decision to reform consciously those behaviors and attitudes that blocked the flow of the Spirit is made. Organically, a greater sensitivity to a Christlike mind is groomed in this daily reflection, and a gradual interior transformation can be seen in the person's choices in the practical aspects of life. Ignatius recommends this exercise be done at noon and at the end of the day for greatest effectiveness.

Directed Eight-Day Retreats

Each Jesuit is asked to make an eight-day silent, directed retreat annually to attend to any disordered or distracted aspects of his life and reorient himself towards Christ. For all of us, the active life can take its toll and, even with the best of intentions, dull our attentiveness to God. Ignatius knew the necessity of regular, systematic reflective time done in dialogue with Scripture and a skilled director.

The yearly retreat, which he advocates for lay and religious alike, allows for a deliberate time of dwelling with Scripture texts selected by a trained retreat director and checking in with Christ in a deeper way than a busy life might afford. On an eight-day directed retreat, at least three separate hours of silent, Scripture-based prayer leads the retreatant into a deeper contemplative grounding in relationship with Christ. It is from this that a renewed dedication and discernment in daily life can occur.

Thirty Days of Spiritual Exercises

At least twice in a Jesuit's formation, both initially as a novice and later during a "second novitiate" or tertianship, Ignatius recommends the Thirty-day Scriptural Retreat. Four "weeks" of spiritual exercises in a carefully crafted progression, the exercitant (the one doing the "exercises") prays through meditations on God's gift in creation, our disordered response and sin towards that gift, and contrition with the examination of conscience. Incorporated is a decision-making for or against Christ and his way, and a systematic dwelling with his life, suffering, death, and resurrection. All of this is meant to serve the purpose of "discernment" of a life's direction. Scriptural passages are provided in an ordered way to maximize the experience of parallel movements that Ignatius himself had experienced in his own process of in-depth conversion.

This process involves the careful accompaniment of a skilled spiritual director, who knows the exercises and can guide the exercitant. Within this deep and intense process, contemplation and intimacy with Christ is experienced. This intimate encounter with Christ assists and clarifies for the exercitant which life direction is most congenial and collaborative with the will of the Holy Spirit.

An alternative form of the thirty-day format of this retreat is the nineteenth-annotation version of the Spiritual Exercises during which the thirty days of meditation are stretched out for several months under the tutelage and guide of a skilled director. For those whose commitments prohibit them from stepping away, this form is becoming increasingly appealing and formative.

In Summary

Ignatian spirituality provides us with guidelines for discernment on life directions, advocates spiritual direction for all people who are serious about their spiritual formation, and provides structures for these to happen. Throughout the world Jesuit Retreat Houses offer skilled directors and environments of silence conducive for those who can extract themselves from their active lives and step apart for deliberate reflection and prayer. In addition, the ongoing practices of spiritual direction and the examen of consciousness reinforce the graces received in life and in retreats.

Questions for Reflection:

- Do you have a way of reviewing and evaluating the way you lived your life each day?
- How is your spirituality one that is both active and contemplative?

Resources for Ongoing Study:

Hellwig, Monika. "The Features of Ignatian Spirituality." *Sojourners* 20:10 (1991).

Hollis, Christopher. *The Jesuits: A History*. New York: Macmillan, 1968.

Ignatius of Loyola. *A Pilgrim's Journey: The Autobiography of Ignatius of Loyola*. Translated by J. Tylenda. Wilmingtom, DE: Glazier, 1985.

Ignatius of Loyola. *Personal Writings*. Translated by Joseph A. Munitiz and Philip Endean. New York: Penguin, 1996.

Meissner, W. W. *Ignatius of Loyola: The Psychology of a Saint*. New Haven, CT: Yale University Press, 1992.

O'Malley, John. *The First Jesuits*. Cambridge: Harvard University Press, 1993.

8

Redemptorist Spirituality
Preachers to the Populace

MANY OF US ARE familiar with the Redemptorist community through parish missions and national publications like *Liguori Magazine*. These ministries stem from a powerful concern for the common person's spiritual development, expressed in the life of their founder, Alphonsus Liguori. Preaching to the uneducated Catholics of his day, Liguori kept his message for ordinary people simple and straightforward, with a focus on the person of Jesus Christ and the profound unconditional love of God. In this chapter we look at the origins of this Redemptorist or Alphonsian spirituality.

The Milieu

The place of Alphonsus Liguori's birth is Marianella, Italy, a suburb of Naples. It is 1696. The Protestant Reformation has split Christianity just over a century ago. In response to the protests of reformers inside and outside the church, a Counter-Reformation movement begins within the Catholic Church. There is great confusion and ignorance with regard to the teachings of Christianity. Illiteracy is rampant. The era is fraught with theologies and spiritualities that focus believers on a God of judgment and rigidity. Heresies like Jansenism and Quietism instill in believers fear of an authoritarian, tyrannical image of God, of judgment and futility.

In Italy the culture is an assortment of small kingdoms with political power held in the cities. The church focuses its energies on city populations, often to the neglect of rural areas. Into these provocative times comes a gifted, intelligent, and earnest young man of noble descent, Alphonsus Liguori.

The Founder

Born the eldest of eight children from a Spanish mother and an Italian commanding officer in the Royal Navy, Alphonsus had many advantages within the social milieu of Naples. Economically and socially established, he completed a double doctorate in civil and church law by the time he was sixteen years old. His nearsightedness and asthma prevented him from military service, so he began his career in the legal profession. As was typical of Italian society, Alphonsus' father had many plans for his first son.

Alphonsus inherited a headstrong authoritarianism from his father and a religious scrupulosity from his mother. Both of these collided inside him in his life direction. After losing an important court case, he despaired of life in the world and laid his nobleman's sword at the feet of the Blessed Virgin Mary, deciding to forego marriage and a legal career for spiritual service. He attended an annual retreat with his father in 1722 and he experienced a radical conversion. At twenty-six, Alphonsus began to study for priesthood and sought spiritual direction from noteworthy directors. The family was not pleased. Not unlike St. Francis of Assisi, this direct intervention by God on this promising son was not seen as suitable or desirable.

Through many physical and psychosomatic illnesses, Alphonsus slowly sought out the direction for his life. His introspection and scrupulosity over his responsibilities nearly crippled him at times. But he was ordained at age thirty and found himself attracted to the poor street people in Naples. Nearly exhausting himself with service to them and concern with his own spiritual life, he left for a rest in the hills of Amalfi. Here, he was struck by the needs of the rural poor in the surrounding countryside. He began to devise ways to meet the spiritual needs, education, and prayer of these simple people through preaching in parish missions. Where the institutional church seemed not able to go, he and his confreres did.

These are the rough origins of the spirituality of the Redemptorists, founded as the Congregation of the Most Holy Redeemer. This man of great zeal and diverse gifts was priest, author, artist, founder, bishop, and man of prayer. He published over one hundred books, aimed at instructing and encouraging in simple language the spirituality of people in the streets. His preaching was aimed at the populace who lacked resources and education. Practical in his thinking, with a sensibility and humor, he conveyed his message in an amiable and benevolent style. A musician and poet, he composed popular hymns still sung throughout Italy.

Significant was his balanced approach to the two prevalent moral stances taken by Dominican rigorists and Jesuit laxists in his day. Liguori's approach appealed to the love of God as central, and avoided the extreme positions of these other two schools of thought. Central to his experience was that of an unconditional, extravagant God of love, who desired a response of love in return. This God desired "nothing but a friendly relationship" with people. God wanted frequent conversation with the faithful. Tenderness and passion marked the image of God that Alphonsus advocated.

Though Alphonsus suffered ill health most of his life, including severe arthritis, he lived ninety-one years, dying in Pagani, Italy, in 1787. His canonization process began only months after his death, and in 1871, he was named a Doctor of the Church. In 1950 he was declared the official patron of moralists and confessors for his brilliant literary approach to pastoral issues.

Spiritual Legacy for Today: Words and Images of Love for All of Us

The primary purpose in the founding of the Redemptorist community was to bring Good News to the poor. Ahead of his time, Liguori affirmed that God's call to holiness was for all people. Two hundred years later, Vatican Council II proclaimed this belief openly in its documents. St. Alphonsus felt that the whole perfection of the human being and all holiness consisted in loving Jesus Christ, and in doing his will. Christ is our Redeemer and the Source of all our good. The legacy of Alphonsus Liguori consisted of this unconditional love of God, emphasis on the redeeming act of Jesus Christ, and encouragement to develop domestic missions to the local populace in need of evangelization. We turn now and ponder this legacy.

The Unconditional Love of God

In "Alphonsian spirituality," holiness of life was directly connected to the unconditional love of God. Two aspects of this love were inferred: the love of God for us and our love for God in return. This legacy challenged the austere images of God of Liguori's era and continued to foster the awareness of Jesus as the physical manifestation of God's love for the world.

Influenced in his youth by the writings of St. Teresa of Avila, whom he referred to as his "second mother," Liguori developed an affective dimension to his prayer and spoke with passion to this God of his love. This he fostered in all of the illiterate poor whom he served in the countryside of Naples. Feeling abandoned by the church, these rural people appeared to be at the mercy of an oppressive God. Liguori introduced the redemptive compassion of God, available to all those who pray.

The Redeeming Act of Jesus Christ

Liguori wrote, "Truly this God of ours is crazy—crazy with love! Has God gone mad in loving us this much?" The unconditional love of God captivated him and he wanted to share that with all those he served. His Italian nature was smitten with a God who loved so much that he became food for us and died for us. Thus, the redeeming act of Jesus Christ was central to his preaching and his moral instruction. This was powerful news to those who were downtrodden or ignored. Redemption was unequivocally offered to all. Each person was a beneficiary of this extravagant love of God, incarnated in the person of Jesus Christ. For a people who felt unloved and neglected, a God who loved so passionately was a comfort and a strength. Alphonsus Liguori radiated this fabulous love of a crazy God.

Domestic Missions

As a response to the Counter-Reformation, Catholicism saw a need to evangelize and upgrade the knowledge levels of people who lacked any formal education. This meant that there was a need for missionaries to

Part III: Ministerial and Active Apostolic Spirituality

the local church. While many Redemptorists would go to other foreign lands, the initial population that Alphonsus Liguori chose to address was the neighbor nearest him. Evangelization of Europe became a primary focus for early Redemptorists. These domestic missions were valued equally as the missions abroad. Preaching to local populations was a means to catechize and correct the lax or ill-informed perspectives of poorly educated people. Liguori was adamant that this population be addressed and responded to through missions devoted to their conversion.

Contemporary Spiritual and Pastoral Contributions

Instruction in prayer continues to be a gift given by the Redemptorist community. With the unconditional love of God and the response of love for God in return as the central spiritual principle of "Alphonsian spirituality," the contributions of the Redemptorists can be seen as a continuation of this awareness and appreciation in today's world. Contemporary believers will find down-to-earth wisdom and practical applications in the legacy of Alphonsus Liguori. Contributions that we will explore from the Alphonsian tradition are practical piety, spiritual and educational resources for the common person, and evangelizing endeavors that prefigure the next centuries' development of a refreshed missionary thrust.

Practical Piety

Alphonsian spirituality encourages people to practice concrete acts of piety and charity. The pious devotions of meditating on the crib, the cross, and the tabernacle are spiritual practices for everyday life. The Stations of the Cross originate with Liguori and his booklet on *The Way of the Cross* continues to sell worldwide, providing inspiration to many during the holy time of Lent and Good Friday.

Prayer is essential for growth in the spiritual life. From this vantage point many forms of prayer are taught and supported by the Redemptorist preachers. Central to Redemptorist spirituality is the Eucharist, whether reverenced during the Mass or outside of it. Alphonsus strongly advocates the daily practice of meditation and reflection on the Word of God. Habitual practice of these devotions can raise up an awareness of the affective dimension of prayer. To awaken the affections of the heart towards God in prayer is a highly valued tenet from Alphonsus' spiritual life. He hoped to foster this same capacity in the common persons among whom he and his confreres ministered.

Resources for the Common Person

Continuing to minister to those who lack resources for their spiritual growth, the Redemptorist community provides preaching resources through missions and printed material from their publishing houses that distribute to many parishes and persons throughout the world. Publications are produced to meet the needs of those whose lives are busy, yet value input for their spiritual journey. Publishing short tracts and leaflets as well as longer spiritual texts, Liguori Press promotes the work of their founder, after whom they are named. Many of these materials are intentionally kept minimal in cost to allow accessibility for all strata of society.

With a concern for the parishioner in the pew, Redemptorists also continue to visit parishes and preach parish missions as a major ministry. This evangelizing service assists in the updating of parishioners' theology and provides inspiration for a deepening of faith and a cultivation of active spiritual vitality.

Evangelizing Endeavors

Missionary zeal was a strong characteristic of Liguori's spirituality. It was this dedication that enabled him to make the controversial step of leaving the comfortable life of a popular preacher in Naples and set out as an itinerant missionary to the peasants and shepherds right outside the gates of the city. The "most abandoned" were those to whom he felt called and, while he was attracted to China, where many of his friends were missioned, he knew that right outside the city gates of Naples were those who needed his attention.

Alphonsus Liguori maintained his missionary work in his own back yard in Italy, but he also preached with the Propaganda priests, many of whom would go to the foreign missions. As the community matured, many Redemptorists went beyond their home geography to serve the needs of the poor in other countries. The American church was stabilized in part by the contribution of Redemptorists who came and settled in Cincinnati and Pittsburgh. From there they spread to New York, Baltimore, and Maryland.

Part III: Ministerial and Active Apostolic Spirituality

By 1902 the Baltimore province was ready to send out missionaries of her own to Puerto Rico and the Caribbean. St. Louis sent missionaries to the Amazon and Thailand. Others went to Nigeria. The preaching went far beyond the perimeters of Naples as a result of that original zeal of one small man. Over five thousand, six hundred Redemptorists serve as missionaries at the current time.

In Summary

Preaching the love of God through written word in publishing or through the spoken word in missions, the Redemptorists continue to carry the religious conviction of their founder. Concern for evangelization of people in the pew worldwide has motivated the Redemptorists to address these needs creatively. Ahead of his time, Alphonsus Liguori dedicated his life to the development of holiness in all believers. The Redemptorists strive to foster that same reality in these post-Vatican II days.

Questions for Reflection:

- What do you understand the word "evangelization" to mean?
- Do you have any acts of piety that you personally value and practice?

Resources for Ongoing Study:

Lowery, Daniel L. *St. Alphonsus Liguori: His Spiritual Legacy.* St. Louis: Liguori, 1987.
Liguorian: A Commemorative Issue 84:8 (August 1996).
Billy, Dennis, C.Ss.R. *Plentiful Redemption: An Introduction to Alphonsian Spirituality.* Liguori: Liguori, 2001.
Swanston, Hamish. *Celebrating Eternity Now: A Study in the Theology of St. Alphonsus Liguori.* Liguori: Liguori, 1995.
Jones, Fredrick, C.Ss.R. *Alphonsus de Liguori: The Saint of Bourbon Naples 1696–1787.* Dublin: Gill & MacMillian, 1991.

9

Salesian Spirituality
Living the Compassion of Jesus in Society

WHILE FAMILIARITY WITH SALESIAN spirituality may be minimal to many, most contemporary Catholics have heard of St. Francis de Sales, who pioneered in support of lay devotion in the early seventeenth century. At his side was St. Jane de Chantal, foundress of the religious community of the Visitation of Holy Mary, known as the Visitandines, which first espoused Salesian spirituality in a novel form appropriate for women who, because of life circumstances, could not enter the cloister. Following upon this foundation came other religious communities of men and women, who were inspired by the spirituality of these two saints: the Salesians of St. John Bosco, the Missionaries of St. Francis de Sales, the Oblates of Francis de Sales, and the Salesian Sisters of Mary Immaculate, all founded long after Francis de Sales' death.

What was so magnetically attractive about the Salesian tradition that allowed it to flourish centuries after the deaths of these two amazing people? Francis and Jane's approach fostered a spirituality of the heart, which revolved around an intimate relationship with Jesus in the world. Let us explore the era that produced these two powerful saints and generated a remarkable devotional spirituality for the world.

Part III: Ministerial and Active Apostolic Spirituality

The Milieu

At the turn of the seventeenth century, incredible changes had occurred within the European continent. New nation states had emerged after a long period of bloody battles. Scientific discoveries by Galileo and Copernicus were challenging the assumptions of geography and cosmology. Western philosophy was being reshaped through new thinkers and encounters with other religious traditions. Reformed Christianity had divided the Christian world into those with a Roman affiliation and those who followed the Protestant evangelizers. Within Catholicism, the Council of Trent spawned a militant reform to address aberrations. A new spiritual energy was manifesting in new religious communities and great religious leaders of saintly quality.

The Founders

As if in response to the torn heart of a previously united Christianity, a new spirituality of the heart was being born in the persons of Francis de Sales (1567–1622) and Jane Frances Fremyot (1572–1641). In France, Francis was born into wealth and privilege, the son of a Savoyard duke, university educated in law, theology, philosophy, and rhetoric. Eventually, a spiritual crisis would lead him to take a stand as advocate for a God of love, which he had experienced intensely in his youth. This would lead him to priesthood and the Bishop's chair in Geneva. He would be sought after for spiritual direction and theological instruction.

Jane was of French origin, born of a Dijonese lawyer and raised to assume her role as Baroness de Chantal, wife, mother, and member of the rising noble class. She was widowed early and raised the surviving four of her six children alone, while attempting to actualize a single-minded passion for God, a conviction that brought many to her door for direction as well.

Initially, Jane took spiritual direction from Francis de Sales, but soon she became his colleague in the spiritual journey, challenging him in mutual concern. Together they formed a partnership that is recorded in the many letters of spiritual direction that passed between them. In response to the needs of their times, their vision would incarnate in the Visitandines, a community of women whose age, health, or commitments to family precluded them entering a rigorous cloister. The original intention was to form a community that felt drawn to religious commitment, served the poor and disadvantaged, but allowed the members to become "daughters of prayer" while attending to the realities of their lives. They would build up the society and infuse it with a spirit of true devotion, allowing laity to realize their spiritual aspirations.

As parents of the Salesian tradition, Francis and Jane contributed a vitality that deeply impacted their world. The theme of Salesian spirituality was "Live Jesus!" which was invoked as their motto on the letterhead of their correspondence. Central to their spiritual school was the call to imitate Christ through gentle and humble witness in the world. No longer did persons have to leave the world in order to realize a spiritual call. The Salesian tradition invited them to incarnate the gentle love of Jesus in active lives, rooted in prayer and daily devotion.

Spiritual Legacy for Today: A Spirituality of the Heart

Francis de Sales and Salesian spirituality emphasized the centrality of the human heart. The devout life involved one that included the affective dimension. Incredibly crucial and attractive for believers was the emphasis on the heart within the spiritual maturation process. Therefore, the legacy of Salesian spirituality involves their approach to spirituality using the language of the heart, the call to the devout life, and the call to practice humility as a part of an active ministerial life, and how these make up a Christian humanism that is pertinent to modern Christianity. We shall reflect on each of these principles as they contribute to their legacy.

Language of the Heart

Appealing to so many people was this language of the heart that de Sales used in writing and speaking about the spiritual life. The heart was the primary symbol that Francis de Sales used to describe human love for God. He inspired his listeners with his passion for Christ, speaking eloquently of the heart opening to divine love. Between the human and the divine, a union of two hearts could take place. Slowly the human heart expanded in its transformative encounter with the heart of God. The pulsating, vibrant human heart underwent a conversion in its core.

Part III: Ministerial and Active Apostolic Spirituality

The Devout Life

Francis de Sales' most memorable spiritual masterpiece is his book, *Introduction to the Devout Life*. It was written as a clear response to needs of his time, encouraging a solid approach to the pursuit of spiritual perfection. A spiritual classic, this writing was meant to instruct earnest laymen and laywomen on how to integrate the call to holinesss with their ordinary lives. It incorporated a spirituality of the heart around the practices of devotion and prayer.

Spirituality of the heart began with an interior orientation, which lead to a gradual external reformation. The heart was the source of actions. As the heart was, so were the actions, according to Francis de Sales. The devout life began as an interior practice and was personalized in a visible way in one's duties of life according to the limits of the person's circumstances. The spiritual life was not intrusive upon one's state in life, but organically germinated from the core of the person's being. De Sales showed exceptional awareness of the human condition in this writing, proposing practical ways to develop the life of Christian prayer within the limits that were reflected in active lay life.

Practicing the Life of Humility

Holiness of life was available to all. It was not evidenced in radical asceticism or heroic acts of external mortification, but in the extremely moderate daily acts of self-surrender, charity, and faithful prayer. The Salesian tradition stressed interiority, yet expressed this in practicing the life of the humble Jesus. The spiritual tradition of Francis de Sales and Jane de Chantal was marked by apostolic zeal, love, and devotion. It was out of this conviction that the injunction to "Live Jesus" emerged. To live the gentle love of Jesus was the epitome of Salesian spirituality.

Christian Humanism

De Sales' profound respect for the human person has often been referred to as "Salesian optimism." He believed in the human person. Without overlooking the reality of human weakness, de Sales was convinced that each person had the natural and supernatural resources needed for sanctity of life. His Christian humanism was ahead of its time. In Francis'

Salesian Spirituality

mind every person was fundamentally oriented towards God in body and in spirit. Naturally inclined towards love, the realization of the human person's dignity and fullness could be actualized through routine acts of daily life. The devout life was possible for ordinary persons through a Christ-centered simplicity and practical mysticism.

Contemporary Spiritual and Pastoral Contributions

Contemporary believers will find great resources within the Salesian tradition to nourish their spiritual lives. Contributions from within the Salesian family include major literary documentation on spiritual direction, the advocacy for holiness for the laity, and the example of the viability of mutual spiritual friendship between women and men.

Spiritual Direction

A treasure trove of spiritual and pastoral insight comes down to present generations through the bevy of letters left behind by both St. Francis de Sales and St. Jane de Chantal. These missives advise and guide the recipient on ways to move deeper in the spiritual life. Their instructions are a part of the rich legacy left behind that can benefit contemporary seekers. Persons hungry for a word of direction can still access the insights of Francis and Jane in texts and in the collection of letters amassed through the years. The record of their correspondence reveals that they were equally invested through their spiritual friendship in the spiritual journey of each other. Strong advocates of spiritual direction for every person, they rarely turned people searching for God away.

Advocacy for Holiness for the Laity

Significant to this is the endorsement of holiness for the laity. De Sales uplifts his lay inquirers to God's desire for them. The parents of Salesian spirituality are intimate, practical, and sensitive to the realities of persons living in the middle of the world, actively engaged with the affairs of lay and religious life. The spirituality of de Sales and de Chantal acknowledges the possibility of holiness within that busyness. They anticipate the wisdom of the Second Vatican Council by over three hundred years. They advocate a holiness of life that is meant for all people. Their prescriptions for moving into deeper intimacy with God include a devotional life with a spirituality that nurtures the heart and encourages human relationships that are supportive of that. This felt sense of God within the person's heart radiates out into society and beyond. De Sales and de Chantal bless the world with this legacy of inclusion and transformation.

The Viability of Mutual Spiritual Friendship Between Women and Men

Authentic spiritual friendship between men and women has often been looked at askance within Christian history. Examples of men and women who struggled to support each other spiritually are very much a part of the story of Christian fidelity, but often critics will cite couples whose attempts were seriously marred by relational impropriety or eccentricity.

Francis de Sales and Jane de Chantal challenge the assumption that a solely spiritual friendship between men and women is impossible. Their relationship is one that was mutually supportive of the spiritual life of the other. They confront their attachment to one another, deal with the longing for God that they shared, and engage in numerous ministerial projects as a team. Their responsibilities separate them geographically most of their lives, but a "bond of perfection" seals their devotion to God and each other. Their love for each other is always surrounded by the love of God, which keeps them focused on their ultimate desire.

For men and women today, the candid disclosures of Francis and Jane in their letters to one another can serve as a guide and support in living intimate, spiritual friendship. Needing models of healthy relationship that recognizes and supports spiritual development, people today can gain a great deal of inspiration and insight from the candid correspondence between these two sages.

In Summary

Francis de Sales' extensive correspondence earned him the title of "patron of journalists." He has also been named a Doctor of the Spiritual Life, frequently referred to as "the Doctor of Divine Love." This love was so impressive that it inspired St. John Bosco two hundred years later to name his community after St. Francis de Sales. The Salesians of St. John Bosco aspired to live the devotional life in the Salesian tradition. The community ministered to youth throughout the world, believing that more good will result by using a gentle, encouraging approach that gradually persuades young people. This approach was strikingly counter-cultural in an era of corporal punishment and abuse.

The Salesians are the third largest religious family in the world, behind the Jesuits and the Franciscans. The dynamism of their spiritual tradition, its language of the heart, its open support of human relationships in the spiritual journey, and its optimistic approach to human potential make the tradition very attractive to contemporary persons. The Christian humanism of Francis de Sales and Jane de Chantal speaks of hope to present generations and encourages the gradual, practical transformation of the world through personal integration and devotion. The Salesian tradition continues to honor the zeal of its founders in preaching through action and attitude, an alternative to solipsism and alienation for believers today.

Questions for Reflection:

- Have you ever experienced spiritual friendship with another person?
- Does anyone in your life seem to be a soulmate for you?

Resources for Ongoing Study:

Sales, Francis de. *Introduction to the Devout Life*. Translated by John K. Ryan. New York: Doubleday, 1982.

Thibert, Peronne Marie, translator. *Francis de Sales, Jane de Chantal: Letters of Spiritual Direction*. Classics of Western Spirituality Series. New York: Paulist, 1988.

Wright, Wendy. *The Bond of Perfection: Jeanne de Chantal and Francois de Sales*. New York: Paulist, 1985.

10

Marist Spirituality
A Marian Missionary Style

WITHIN CATHOLIC CHRISTIAN SPIRITUALITY, devotion to the Blessed Virgin Mary has swelled at different times throughout the ages. Few communities of religious have taken Marian spirituality to heart as completely as "The Society of Mary," known also as the Marists. Faithful men and women have realized their religious vocations as brother, sister, and priest for over a hundred and fifty years through the apostolic thrust and missionary zeal of the Marist communities. Let us look at their origins.

The Milieu

The milieu was nineteenth-century France. For a century or more, a flurry of religious fervor had swept the region, generating exceptional enthusiasm for spiritual endeavors. Religious foundations rapidly cropped up, and interest in the new territories that had been discovered in the explorations of the New World of the 1700s surged. Missionary congregations were founded to address the spiritual needs of the varied peoples in these areas. Educational, medical, and social-service institutions were built by the church throughout Europe and the Americas to respond to the social consciousness being raised by popes, theologians, and founders. The new

Christian social doctrine inspired many laity to overtly dedicate themselves to serving the needy through charitable acts and institutions.

New forms of religious life also emerged. Women's groups struggled to do apostolic ministry while shackled with the rules of monasticism. Secular priests banded together to form societies working on a common apostolate but technically not "religious" in their style of living. The ministry took precedence over personal perfection or rigidly scheduled periods of prayer.

The Founders

Not a lot of written material is available when researching the founders of apostolic groups like the Marists. Many were too busy working to write their thoughts and concerns down. Within the Marist family, fortune smiled in the person of Gabriel-Claude Mayet, who copiously recorded the instructions and sayings of one of the founding figures, Father Jean-Claude Colin. The Marist foundation was a corporate experience with many different personalities contributing to its formulation. The energies of Colin, Jean-Claude Courveille, Marcellin Champagnat, and Jeanne-Marie Chavoin coalesced in a project unlike any religious congregation the church had previously seen.

The vision was simple: Mary, like the Mother she was, wanted no one abandoned; all of those from the edge of life should be gathered and cared for, as they were in the early church. This "work of Mary" was to be a multi-branched organization of priests, religious, and laypeople working to gather all into the body of Christ. They intended to follow their model of Mary and support all the forgotten.

While their governance would eventually be split by Rome into separate groups, the Marists still intended to work as a unit to realize this goal. It was a family spirituality initiated by Mary for the good of all her children.

Spiritual Legacy for Today: Collaboration for the Marginalized

Mary was the inspiration for the Marist community from the very beginning. Following her lead and feeling as if they were "the first children of Mary," called to serve Christ as a family united by her, the Marists were attracted to this enterprise because they felt it would make a difference in the lives of others and themselves. Though not exclusively missionary, a spirituality emerged that would take them to the marginalized in faraway lands and inspire them to provide educational services for those at home. This "something new" would include everyone and push mercy to an extreme.

The legacy of these founders of the Marist community was evidenced in a social thrust that incorporated an integration of all vocational calls, an acknowledgment of the needs of the times that governed and shaped the missionary endeavor, and a reformulation of the church under the guidance of Mary. We shall examine each of these elements briefly now.

A Social Thrust

A social thrust distinguished the Marist project from many of the spiritualities prior to the nineteenth century. The spirituality of monastics and mendicants had been responses to the needs of their times, and the Marian missionaries now supplied something for which the era was desperate—an integrated approach of clerics and laity, men and women moving into social action with a Marian concern. While the spiritual path included holiness of life and prayer, it also included an active involvement and response to the social needs of the people. As missionaries, Marists readied themselves to engage in this social reality, even as they fostered their spiritual life of prayer.

The Needs of the Times

Factored in to the call of the community were the needs of the times. As such, a certain urgency developed with the community. "The times" were those of the cultural shift of the Enlightenment in Western civilization, complete with alienation, indifference, and materialism. Atheism was also a new phenomenon that was growing. The French Revolution had moved a society towards freedom, equality, and fraternity but had employed bloodshed in many situations to enforce it. The church's heavy-handed response was equally questionable. Society needed something else, grounded in mercy.

Marist Spirituality

Reformulation of the Church under the Guidance of Mary

Reading these signs, a new church was needed. If this possibly was the prelude to the end of the world, the world needed to be transformed into a model that gathered and welcomed all. The Marist vision was that of a church reborn, conquering pride and unbelief with a faith that was purified and simplified like that of its beginnings. A return and reformulation of the early church, appropriately revised for today and under the same guidance of Mary, was necessary.

Contemporary Spiritual and Pastoral Contributions

The contribution of the Marist family is pluriform. All of the founders speak of the "Work of Mary" as being something bigger than the Society of Mary. They are enablers of Mary's work to be done in this world. The ministry is in the world, inclusive of the laity, and emphasizes mercy and compassion. Each of these deserves attention at this point.

Mary's Work in the World

The conviction that Mary's work is in the world was a sharp departure from many of the spiritualities of the day. A contribution that the Marists make is a willingness to work in the world for its transformation, never rejecting it as somehow inferior. Marist spirituality is a spirituality of the marketplace, enmeshed with the concerns of people in reality. Theirs is not a utopian, idealized world of the future but one that they are engaged in lovingly and fully. As Mary loves this creation, so Marists work for its good.

Inclusivity of the Laity

A strong inclusiveness toward the laity also characterizes a unique gift of the Marist tradition. From the beginning laity were included and validated in their contribution to the community and the enterprise. The image of the multi-branched tree serves as a reminder to many of the diversity and inclusivity of this community. Laity are always integral to the endeavor and a part of the full Marist vision. They are no mere afterthought but belong within the whole of the Marist family. Along with this, welcome becomes a primary feature of Marist houses. Hospitality and inclusion are valued by Marist communities as signs of this acceptance and attitude of welcome.

Mercy and Compassion

It is symbolic that the first twenty Marists made their Professions on the feast of Our Lady of Mercy. Mercy and compassion guide the approach of the Marist mission as a living incarnation of Marian concern. The language of the Society of Mary is distinctly feminine in tone, using words like "uniting," "harmonizing," and "gathering." This emphasis portrays a more feminine side of God, church, and religious service that is not perceived as powerful, controlling, or administrative. Rather, the approach is one of simplicity, mercy, fellowship, and compassion. Caring for the fragile with sensitivity undergirds the ministerial philosophy of the Marist community.

In Summary

The strong devotion to Mary undergirds the spirituality of the entire Marist community, men and women alike. Together they form a family of ministers who generously serve the needy. Their collaboration and compassion truly mark them as examples of Mary's presence in the world. As practitioners of hospitality and welcome, they follow in her steps as people who care for the world that her son came to heal.

Questions for Reflection:

- Does Mary, the mother of Jesus, play a role of any kind in your spiritual life?
- Is there a feminine dimension to your own spirituality?

Resources for Ongoing Study:

Hosie, Stanley. *Anonymous Apostle*. New York: William Morrow, 1967.

Larkin, Craig. *A Certain Way: An Exploration of Marist Spirituality*. Rome: Center for Marist Studies, 1995.

McMahon, Frederick. *Strong Mind, Gentle Heart*. Parramatta: Macarthur, 1988.

PART IV
Missionary Spirituality

Introduction

THE DEVELOPMENT OF A specifically missionary spirituality was a complex one, controversial in many ways but one that was also fraught with disaster, danger, and disillusion. Many of the active ministerial communities mentioned in Part III did missionary outreach both on the home front and abroad. In fact, the missionary movement beyond Europe was initially championed by Jesuits, Franciscans, and Dominicans who carried their apostolic zeal for teaching, preaching, and evangelizing to new worlds. Their stories depicted heroic courage, conviction, and commitment in their attempts to widen the tent of the church. Their radical consent to travel and convert tribal peoples cannot be discounted in any way. From the sixteenth to eighteenth centuries, they carried the standard for the missionary apostolate.

But later in the nineteenth century a new breed of missionary congregation emerged whose sole purpose of existence was missionary life. This fourth category is a school of spirituality that decidedly focuses on evangelization of peoples who had no familiarity with the Christian message. In Part IV we will focus on congregations that exclusively were formed to travel to foreign countries to serve peoples beyond their home countries. Under the umbrella as missionaries, these congregations were designated ambassadors of Christianity, carrying the Good News to cultures and societies that were predominantly new to the Christian message.

Historically, missionary spirituality grew out of the spiritual impulse to go out with the Gospel vision and better the world. It is as ancient as the Gospel. Like ministerial and active apostolic spirituality, its purpose was to spread the Good News that Jesus preached upon the planet. The initial disciples were Jews from Palestine who were local boys with

Part IV: Missionary Spirituality

good hearts and a powerful firsthand experience of Jesus Christ. They were moved by the Pentecost revelation and burst into the city streets of Jerusalem and the surrounding region to proclaim the news of God's love. The Holy Spirit pushed them out into a larger world with its energy and vitality. Such enthusiasm could not remain in a nonverbal silence, but had to be announced to all who could hear. However, if the spread of the Good News had remained exclusively with them, the larger Gentile world would never have known the Christian message. Teachers with a missionary spirit and energy had to take the story out into a broader world.

Tradition tells us that a few of these first disciples did travel beyond Palestine, carrying the Word. St. Thomas is reputed to have gone east into India. St. Philip is noted for going to Greece and Syria. However, in the first century St. Paul of Tarsus, a Pharisee, was the icon of Christian missionary zeal. The most pronounced missionary thrust within Christianity manifested most obviously in his person and that of his companions, who undertook at least three major missionary journeys to spread the Gospel message not just to faithful Jews in the Roman world, but to people of good faith within the larger Gentile communities.

The initial missionary path was restricted to the known world and peoples of the Middle East and the European continent. Within the first four hundred years of Christian development, the social upheaval and political reconfiguration in these regions determined and deterred Christian expansion. The focus in many ways was stabilization of economies and clarification of doctrinal issues. After the Edict of Milan in 312 CE, Christianity settled into a form of political and ecclesial Christendom, shaping the cultures and societies in which it grew. In the West it provided some safety and security from marauding bands of invaders who caused considerable distress and destruction. While some missionary activity was occurring with Celtic monks traveling to tribes who did not know Christianity on the mainland, a long hiatus of over a thousand years passed in the missionary thrust of Christianity.

A recovery of this missionary drive was triggered by the discovery of territories beyond the European continent by the Spanish, Portuguese, Italian and French in the fifteenth and sixteenth centuries. There was still a need for domestic missionary work within Europe. But the exposure to new places expanded the possibilities for political and ecclesial projects. A fire for carrying the Gospel reignited with the news of expeditions that were carrying explorers to unchurched lands.

Introduction to Part IV

Active ministerial and mendicant communities recognized the need for moving out to these lands and evangelizing the local people. Initially, they accompanied the military and merchants in going into new regions in Asia and the Americas. They were providing religious support for the sailors and colonists on the expeditions. But their objectives were different than those of the military and mercenaries that exploited these territories; missionaries felt called to join in the encounter with new peoples and cultures to spread Christianity.

The missionary chronicle is filled with horror stories of confrontation with tribal authorities, conflict with idolatrous customs, and confusing dictates from Rome that revealed tremendous ignorance. Missionaries died of disease, were killed by potentates, were shipwrecked or drowned at sea. The external demands of existence in harsh climates, hostile communities, and isolation abroad took their toll on the majority of the first generation of this new missionary surge. These hardships cannot be minimized when we look at the long saga of missionary consent.

In the seventeenth century, there was tension between importing Christianity in its primal form versus a form laden with the cultural accretions from the colonial powers. Missionaries struggled in this tension, trying to follow the mandate from the newly formed Propaganda of the Faith to preserve unharmed the customs and manners of the local people while imparting the faith. Respect for the ancient cultures was often compromised by those who could not recognize the value in this diversity, or adapt to it, if it did not violate the morality and doctrine of sound religion. This was not easy to ascertain and many bishops wrestled with the challenges in the culture while waiting for guidance from Rome.

Rome herself gave ambiguous messages and caused great difficulty for many creative missionaries who were attempting to negotiate curious customs and understandings. Having never encountered the types of questions and challenges presented in polygamist cultures or multi-religious communities, the hierarchy fumbled with how to address these provocative practices with fidelity to their understanding of the truth.

An emphasis on raising up a local, indigenous clergy was also placed upon these missionaries by the Propaganda Office. Missionary clergy, while meeting the needs of the newly converted, also tried to prepare aspirants for ordination and service. This was not an easy task. Conflicts and confusion prompted the expulsion and execution of many expatriate clergy and the few indigenous religious that had been educated. This resulted in a lull in missionary effectiveness for over a hundred years.

Then in the nineteenth century a rush of spiritual fervor and fresh energy erupted in an explosion of missionary interest. This energy manifested in communities whose primary focus was service directly to the foreign missions. These women and men intentionally felt called to address the spiritual and societal needs of the local people in distant, developing countries. While the European continent recovered from severe political revolutions and industrial evolutions, faithful missionaries left their home soil specifically to encounter new peoples, cultures, and environments. Their intent was to bring pastoral relief and religious hope to those to whom they went.

The flare of spiritual enthusiasm moved women as well as men to step out bravely and enter into corporal works of mercy in other lands. This was a bold departure from the protective confinement levied upon them previously by the patriarchal system of Rome. These missionary women moved beyond these barriers and addressed the struggles of women and children, especially creating educational and medical facilities to improve the literacy and the lifespan of those in remote areas. They often provided a gentler face in the midst of violent conquests. A veritable force of charitable energy, they witnessed to the validity of their own call as missionaries to meet the needs in distant coasts.

Even in this thumbnail introduction, it is clear that there were many phases in the development of missionary spirituality. While it is impossible to elaborate in this context the complexity of the missionary endeavor, it is important to note that this movement has had many challenges in its ebb and flow historically. The root urge within all phases was that of the Holy Spirit, pushing the envelope of assumptions about Christianity and stretching the structures to incorporate, however slowly, new peoples and mindsets. Finding God in all things and all peoples broke open the insularity of the church, previously confined to Western European lands and perceptions. Despite the mixed attitudes and approaches to mission, missionary spirituality opened the Eurocentric mind of the church to a broader horizon.

This energetic missionary thrust took on a new face in the 1960s when the Second Vatican Council endorsed a mission approach of presence versus conversion. With a new respect for the spiritual elements hidden in the cultures to which evangelizers were sent, Catholic Christian missionaries adopted approaches that met the local populations where they were, acknowledging the giftedness already there. Missionaries turned their focus to the holistic formation of those they served, becoming concerned with their social needs and development, as well as with their religious formation. It was a mission of presence versus proselytizing and conversion.

The missionary spirit of the nineteenth century produced hundreds of new congregations devoted to the global community. Communities of men and communities of women collaborated in bringing their skills to nations that lacked literacy or were victimized by loss of land and property. Clergy, religious, and laity found in mission lands a new opportunity to work together, too, and join their efforts and talents in a living witness of Gospel solidarity. In this section we will dwell with three groupings that have spread the Gospel and administered justice and mercy in developing countries, namely, the Spiritans or Holy Ghost congregation and the Catholic Foreign Mission Society of America and the Foreign Mission Sisters of Saint Dominic, known as Maryknoll, and the Society of African Missions.

11

Spirituality of the Spiritans
Missionaries and Educators to the Poor and Abandoned

Many in the United States may not recognize the name of "The Spiritans" as it is associated with the Holy Ghost Fathers. Not surprisingly, many Americans may not be familiar with this community at all because the spirituality and ministry of the Spiritans takes them abroad as missionaries and educators. This mission community boasts two founders, who lived one hundred and fifty years apart. When the original vision of Claude Poullart des Places in 1703 met the spirit and heart of Francis Libermann in 1848, a new missionary energy and dedication formalized itself into the Congregation of the Holy Ghost, today referred to as "The Spiritans." Each of these men's vitality continues to thrive in missionaries who populate Africa, the Americas, and the Caribbean. Let us look at the historical roots of this community and the spiritual contribution they continue to offer.

The Milieu

The origins of the Holy Ghost Congregation stem from a spirituality from the late 1600s that fostered a devotion to the Holy Spirit and the Blessed Mother. Throughout France preachers and people in the pews practiced

Part IV: Missionary Spirituality

a serious attentiveness to the promptings of the Holy Spirit, attempting to live in fidelity to God. This spiritual influence permeated schools and communities and eventually congealed in the formation of a loose-knit movement of clergymen.

The Founders

Claude Poullart des Places (1679–1709), a millionaire's son and a brilliant lawyer, was steeped in this spirituality, and he left his affluent life to study theology in the early 1700s. During his studies, he began to provide food and lodging to fellow theology students who lacked financial resources. Gradually, the Jesuit bursar of the seminary began to assist him. Des Places was led unintentionally to found a seminary and write a governing rule for those in residence. He consecrated this little band to the Holy Spirit and the Blessed Virgin, founding it in 1703 with strict requirements for admission and a staunch spirituality as its base.

Organization was secondary to charism and educational excellence at this point in their founding. When des Places died at twenty-four years of age, only two years after his own ordination, the only written documentation to guide this fledgling group, devoted to serving the poor and abandoned, was a series of house rules for students. The initial foundation of the Holy Ghost Congregation revolved around the education of poor clerics in ecclesiastical discipline and love of virtue. They would be ready to serve in positions for which it was difficult to find ministers. A radical zeal accompanied these men and fired their desire to go where no one else would serve.

Loosely formed, they would move into missionary endeavors thirty years later when the historical need added mission territories to the list of preferred poor and abandoned works. Their disciplined lifestyle and commitment to evangelical poverty made them desirable associates for the missions. Still operating as diocesan priests under the jurisdiction of various bishops, many were pulled back from the missions to teach in seminaries because their academic prowess was so admired by those in leadership.

The Congregation existed more as "a movement" than a religious body or formal community for over a hundred and fifty years. Within that time it suffered greatly through suppression during the French

Revolution. Schools were closed and buildings confiscated. Teetering on its own without good leadership, the congregation devoted to the training of clergy deteriorated.

New possibilities emerged gradually after the conversion of Jacob Libermann (1802–1852), the son of an orthodox rabbi of Saverne, France. Jacob, who took the name "Francis," disappointed his father's dreams of his son's succession as rabbi, when he was baptized in 1826 in Paris. Spurned by his father, Francis threw himself into his new religious identity, carrying with him a pious Jewish self-discipline and advanced education in the Torah and Talmud. In 1827 he began to study theology with the hopes of ordination.

Libermann was not a physically robust young man. Health difficulties had plagued him throughout his life. Epilepsy excluded him from advancing into major orders with the Sulpicians but he continued to deepen in his spiritual life as he studied. In 1837 his spiritual genius was recognized and he accepted the invitation to become assistant novice master for the Eudists. Two years later, hearing the Holy Spirit's call, he went to Rome to found a new congregation, dedicated to the Holy Heart of Mary, with the purpose of serving the needs of the black slaves and promoting missionary outreach.

The two communities coexisted with some tension for a while. But similarities and need began to tie them together. Libermann's ministry for over fourteen years had been the formation of future priests. He brought the wisdom from those years of service and applied it towards the education of clergy for the foreign missions, wedding the original purpose of the Spiritans with that of the Holy Heart of Mary.

In 1848, an amalgamation of the two communities occurred, strengthening both groups with a stability and recognition that only benefitted the ministry. Together they fostered solid spiritual leadership within the church in the new lands to which they would go. The dual interest in the missions and the education of clergy would both be respectfully achieved.

Spiritual Legacy for Today: Evangelical Availability

Both des Places and Libermann attended to the directives of the Holy Spirit within the historical milieux in which they lived. Their great conviction

Part IV: Missionary Spirituality

that the Holy Spirit spoke through the persons, places, and events of life was a common bonding between them, despite the century and a half that separated their lives. Availability to the Spirit's invitation became a key feature of the zealous men who gathered around each of these men. The radical willingness to listen faithfully and respond wholeheartedly to the Holy Spirit within the concrete circumstances of life characterized their charism and their spiritual approach. Part of the legacy of des Places and Libermann, therefore, included evangelical availability, evangelical poverty, and active self-disposal to the Holy Spirit.

Evangelical Availability

Evangelical availability contained two aspects: availability before God and availability before human beings. Each of these was a facet of the one availability, breaking down the split between the spiritual life and apostolic service. The first implied a call to holiness, a willingness to be open to a spiritual life of prayer and devotion to the presence of God. The second required openness to the world through which the Spirit speaks and an awareness that the continuous presence of God is housed within this world. This ongoing availability to God undergirded all apostolic activity. A response of generous openness to God played out in the service to fellow human beings.

Evangelical availability was a principle strongly encouraged by Libermann, He saw it as the foundational principal from which effective missionary work took its form. The heart of the true missionary must be willing to be available to God and human, responding in great generosity and holiness of life.

Evangelical Poverty

This double availability involved evangelical poverty, incorporating both a material poverty and a poverty of spirit. The first entailed a moderate approach to the goods of the earth communally and individually. Material necessities of life could not be an obstacle to the Spiritan's availability to the needs of the abandoned. A modest respect and a limit placed upon material wealth freed the Spiritan to go forth to serve wherever needed. Spiritual poverty entailed ongoing openness to the Spirit to go wherever

Spirituality of the Spiritans

the Spirit led. Human voices often revealed the Holy Spirit's directives. Openness to the ever-changing situations of life required detachment from internal possessiveness that might hamper the embrace of new challenges. Poverty of spirit and simplicity of life were two sides of the same coin out of which the Spiritan went forth to serve the mission.

Actively Being in Touch with the Holy Spirit

Evangelical availability invited contemporary people to live gracefully in touch with the Holy Spirit within the mobility and the change of the modern world. In the spirituality of the day, a new interest in the third Person of the Trinity had emerged. This devotion to the Holy Spirit prompted a response of willingness to listen to the invitation of the Spirit and to follow its lead. Active engagement with the Holy Spirit required an attentiveness that allowed Spiritans to change course, if so directed. They were disposed to go where the Holy Spirit charged them to go and meet a need.

Libermann actively modeled this internal self-disposal to the Spirit, even though he was never allowed to move on to mission countries. Dying at age fifty, he had placed his entire adult life in the hands of the Spirit. His availability had an evangelical repercussion that spread through his confreres to continents and communities beyond his wildest imagination. The missionary thrust of the Holy Ghost Congregation took Libermann's vision and carried it far beyond European soil.

Contemporary Spiritual and Pastoral Contributions

The original fire that melded the spirituality of the Spiritans to the Holy Ghost was strongly influenced by the Jesuits, who encouraged fidelity to the Holy Spirit. That active, engaged approach to the world and God's word spoken therein formed a foundational approach that propelled the congregation into an active apostolic spirituality. Francis Libermann continued this involvement, challenging the notion that God could only be found in a monastic approach to God. This other approach to the spiritual life supported a practical union with God within everyday life.

This continues to be a part of the legacy that the Spiritan founders and community bring to contemporary believers. We can find God within the reality of active lives. Other contributions that the Spiritan

Part IV: Missionary Spirituality

congregation continues to offer us include a valuing of experience, flexibility, personal dignity, and democratic leadership. Let us look at these gifts for contemporary believers.

A Valuing of Experience

"Look for God in the ever-changing situations of life." These words governed the life of the pious Jew, and Francis Libermann carried this awareness into his life as a Christian and as a Spiritan. His spiritual instruction carried with it a respect for the Holy Spirit's movement within the concrete realities of life. Paying attention to a person's experience was a practice that Libermann not only supported but taught his followers to apply.

With this perspective he manifested great reverence for the many different ways that the Holy Spirit acted in people's lives. He was attentive to the multifarious movements of the Spirit in individuals and communities. This respectful attentiveness characterized his work in spiritual direction and his writings to those working far away.

This practice of being attentive to and valuing the experience of people in their spiritual journey is one from which today's Christian can gain a lot of insight. Respect for this diversity can give people today a broadened perspective that can inhibit judgment and rigidity.

Flexibility

With his regard for individual human experience as the vehicle through which the Holy Spirit worked, Libermann encouraged flexibility. A certain practicality accompanied his profound spiritual grounding. Libermann's experience with many seminarians had taught him the value of remaining open to change within the decisions and directions that the congregation should go. In contrast to the inflexibility he witnessed in the clergy in 1848, he stressed a mobility that prevented missionaries from getting stuck in a groove. He advocated adaptability. He counseled his congregation to continue to see where the Spirit was leading, adjusting themselves creatively to respond to the needs of the times. He advised his men to trust in experience and not get locked in the past, a message that is a solid one for people today as well.

Personal Dignity

Libermann had a profound respect for the personal dignity of each person with which he dealt. This regard for the individual came out of his sensitivity to the diverse ways in which the Holy Spirit called persons. Listening attentively to the nuances of each person's circumstances allowed him to speak with great authority and accuracy in the guidance of those who sought him out.

For contemporary believers, this reverence for the dignity of each person is crucial and Libermann's example in leadership and humility is particularly helpful. The dignity of the human person is one that can be overshadowed by the mandates of business, work, and cultural expectations. Libermann reminds us to maintain a regard for the personal dignity of all human beings, never disregarding this fundamental awareness. We are challenged to foster this despite an aggressive culture which can try to squeeze it out.

Democratic Leadership

Remarkable for his time in ecclesial history, Libermann endorsed the idea that the Holy Spirit spoke through the voices of the majority within the community. These voices needed to be heard and respected. In faithfully listening to the Spirit, each person contributed to the leadership through a faithful, responsible attentiveness.

His openness to change within his own leadership and vision was attested to by his naming of the first constitution of the congregation, which he had written, as "provisional." Even the merging of the two congregations required painstaking skill on Libermann's part to lead the two groups into a cohesive unit. He knew the Spirit could instruct them through experience and change the original understanding to something more appropriate.

This method of leadership, of course, is one that is familiar to us now. Libermann's modeling of this democratic approach to decision making remains a challenge, however, within the church. A respectful and faithful receptivity to the directives of the Holy Spirit continues to be a discipline that stretches the ecclesial community as well as individuals within.

Part IV: Missionary Spirituality

In Summary

With the guidance of the Holy Spirit and the Blessed Mother, the Spiritans carry forth the respectful and responsive attentiveness of their founders. They continue to go forth as missionaries and educators and attest to the powerful belief that God is operative in the world in the concreteness of life. Evangelic availability disposes them to go wherever the Spirit leads them and work for an incarnation of the Gospel in whatever way is demanded of them. The witness of the Spiritan community prompts us to increase our receptivity to the lead of the Holy Spirit in our work, our study, and our homes.

Questions for Reflection:

- What has been your experience of placing yourself in the hands of the Holy Spirit?
- Have you ever felt a tension between a call to serve and giving yourself time for prayer?

Resources for Ongoing Study:

Koren, Henry. *Essays On The Spiritan Charism And On Spiritan History*. Bethel Park, PA: Spiritus, 1990.

———. *To The Ends Of The Earth: A General History of the Congregation of the Holy Ghost*. Pittsburgh: Duquesne University Press, 1983.

Van Kaam, Adrian. *A Light to the Gentiles: The Life Story of the Venerable Francis Libermann*. Lanham, MD: University Press of American, 1985.

12

Maryknoll Spirituality
Missionaries of Presence and Purpose

OF ALL THE COMMUNITIES represented in this text, the only one that was birthed on American soil is the Maryknoll Missionaries. Under their official name as the Catholic Foreign Mission Society of America and the Foreign Mission Sisters of Saint Dominic, Maryknoll is a unique blend of men and women working together as laity, ordained, and religious from all over the world. A young community by ecclesial standards, they are now spread throughout the world with a diverse makeup of nationalities and cultures. Their spirituality is decidedly active, enfleshing zeal and energy for improving a world rife with injustice and need.

The Milieu

The century had just turned from the 1800s to the 1900s when the missionary zeal that began among Protestant youth in the United States began to spread into Catholicism. Immigrants from Ireland, Poland, Austria-Hungary, Germany, and Italy had flooded the new American nation in the previous fifty years, fleeing to escape famine, despair and joblessness. Protestant New England did not look favorably on these newcomers. There was a sense of threat felt with this influx. Not only

Part IV: Missionary Spirituality

were they politically at odds with those coming over in droves but they were religiously different. These new arrivals were Catholic. In New England, an Irish-Yankee tension grew and manifested as discrimination and opposition.

Internationally, early tensions were paving the way for political upheaval on the European continent that would erupt in World Wars, the first devastating one a mere fourteen years away. The first two decades of the twentieth century would also include economic disaster on American shores with the Great Depression. In an isolationist period, these were difficult times to start a new endeavor that would need financing and support for work abroad. But in December 1906, when Mollie Rogers trudged into Fr. James Walsh's dingy office in Boston, all of these challenges were remote and secondary. God was at work in cultivating new relationships to help expand the missionary charism.

The Founders

Mary Josephine Rogers, known as Mollie, was a young Irish-American graduate of Smith College in central Massachusetts. After graduation she had continued her relationship with Smith College by returning to teach zoology there. She had been asked by her Alma Mater to start a women's group for the minority of Catholic women on campus. She felt led to make this group a mission study class, something that previously had only been available to Protestant women at the school. On American soil, within the Protestant community a missionary thrust was already flourishing. The Student Volunteer Movement had already ignited on college campuses, including Smith College, and was manifesting in graduates dedicating several years of service to the foreign missions. Mollie was touched by this enthusiasm and wanted to introduce it to her Catholic colleagues.

At the same time, Fr. James Anthony Walsh, Director of the office of The Society of the Propagation of the Faith, had begun to explore with three other priests in Boston the possibility of founding the Catholic Foreign Mission Board. There was a need to foster priestly vocations for the missions, they felt, and their plan was to bring the mission church into homes of Catholics in their own country. There was a conviction that the American Catholic community was ready to share in the project of the foreign missionary movement. The American Catholic immigrants had settled in and stabilized in their new home. It was time to awaken the American Catholic missionary consciousness.

When Mollie Rogers conferred with Fr. Walsh about her project, he welcomed her and offered his support, inviting her to become involved in his own newly prepared publication, *The Field Afar*. A partnership of sorts formed along with Fr. Thomas Frederick Price, which eventually would flower into a new mission society in the United States. Mollie along with several other women became the editors and production crew for the publication, while Fr. Walsh sought funding, land, and seminarians. Nicknamed "the secretaries," the personal spirituality and dedication of these women would put the publication in homes all across the country, exposing Catholic families to their responsibility to care for a larger world.

The mission society initially focused on the formation of priests as the foundation of the new mission society. This was readily accepted in April 1911 by church authorities in Rome. But the women, too, involved in the work began to gel into a cohesive devout community with Mollie Rogers emerging as the leader. She became known as Mother Mary Joseph with Fr. Walsh as Father General. In later years he would be elevated to that of a Bishop in keeping with his ecclesial responsibilities for those serving abroad.

There were many obstacles, not the least of which was reticence on the part of Rome to admit these fledgling women as vowed religious. Separate governance between the men's community and women's community was demanded and only after three attempts at presenting the women's case before Rome were the Maryknoll Sisters in February 1920 admitted officially as a new congregation.

Thus began the phenomenal process of an immigrant church growing into its own maturity as a mission-sending community. Those who had benefitted from the generosity of other's sharing their faith and building institutions to help them educate, heal, and worship as faithful Catholic Christians in North America now were ready to send workers and resources to other countries where the struggle was reminiscent of their own. Collaboration between priests, brothers, sisters, and laity in direct service beyond their own borders was a radical new phenomenon for the American church.

Part IV: Missionary Spirituality

Spiritual Legacy for Today: Sacrifice and Identification with the Poor

The spirituality of Maryknoll is marked overtly by an American approach to making the world a better place through active involvement with the poor. Moved by the social dimension of the Gospel, Maryknoll missionaries placed themselves directly with the disenfranchised, the marginalized, and those forgotten or abandoned by society. This placement often put them in harm's way. Yet, as missionaries, they were well aware that many had gone before them as martyrs, whose active engagement for the sake of justice had lead them to sacrifice their own safety. Let us look at this legacy that marks the Maryknoll story.

Martyrs

It might sound strange and even bizarre to count martyrs as a gift that a congregation gives to the larger church, but these lives that have been taken unjustly in violence, abuse, and tyranny resound loudly from their graves with the stories of injustice. Martyrdom was recognized by the founders of Maryknoll as a very real possibility for their members. In fact, martyrdom was an important part of the spirituality of these missionaries, who knew the likelihood of loss of life by embarking on journeys where a return home to safety and security was rare.

Maryknoll lost many missionaries through invasions, wars, covert operations, and inhuman acts by the military. Many of these deaths were the result of their work with the oppressed, those shunted to the side of society without a voice. In an attempt to silence them or reduce their authority, death and torture were options chosen by those who opposed them. Whether it was the invasion of China, the death march of Bataan, the torture by the Japanese, or rape and gun shots in El Salvador, the list of Maryknoll missionaries who have lost their lives standing with the people and refusing to leave when instability threatened their work is staggering. Their blood is a huge sacrifice and gift, evidence of a faith that goes beyond the pragmatic or the easy.

Most known by many present day Christians are the four church women, three of whom were Maryknoll missionaries, who were martyred in cold blood by the military in El Salvador. In December 1980, Maryknoll Sisters Ita Ford and Maura Clark and lay Maryknoll missioner

Maryknoll Spirituality

Jean Donovan, along with Ursuline Sister Dorothy Kazel, were raped and assassinated for their direct service with the struggling poor in Central America. Other killings in that country have included Archbishop Oscar Romero in March 1980 and six Jesuit priests and their housekeeper in November 1989. Many of the Maryknoll men and women on mission live in tense and unpredictable situations. Daily they must choose between their own safety and the advocacy they believe in offering the abused of society. These women chose to remain even as threats to their lives increased. Maryknoll's spirituality as a missionary congregation puts them directly at risk, often in places around the globe where instability and injustice require their presence.

Active Engagement for Justice

As evidenced above, central to the Maryknoll charism was the call to right the wrongs of injustice by active engagement with political powers, social structures, and economic inequities that harm many people in mission lands. Maryknoll from its very inception was dedicated as a congregation to address the problems of oppressed people. Their awareness of the social dimension of the Gospel thrust them into situations of need and suffering. Along with an apostolic vision of how the Gospel could look in the lives of Christians throughout the world, these missionaries have rolled up their sleeves to work actively alongside the populations who were discounted or dismissed by the system.

This engagement overseas often surprisingly brought them back to their own soil to challenge political realities that resulted in violence in mission countries. Maryknoll missionaries were significant in their challenge to authorities in their home countries that exacerbated or promoted military aggression in poor nations. An example of this was the challenge levied against the United States military for the role they have played in arming and training military and paramilitary groups in Central America at the U.S. Army's School of the Americas in Fort Benning, Georgia. Through political pressure, the awareness of the American people and government has been raised about the connection between the military in the U.S. and abroad. Many began to ask questions about this alliance and grappled with the consequences of violence and bloodshed that had increased.

Part IV: Missionary Spirituality

Contemporary Spiritual and Pastoral Contributions

Contemporary Christians need the modeling of congregations like Maryknoll to open up a larger world to them. We live in an era when technology brings the news of distant countries and cultures into our homes through television, computers, and radio. To ignore the connection between the many peoples who share this planet is to live disconnected from global relationship and social responsibility. Maryknoll missionaries are conduits for this connection, breaking down hostilities, prejudices, and distance between people of their home countries and those of their hosts. They contribute significantly to our pastoral attentiveness through mission awareness, respect for cultural diversity, and direct service opportunities for laity and associate religious. Let us examine each of these gifts.

Mission Awareness

Many an American Catholic child growing up in the 1900s readily recalls being captivated by photographs and stories from a Maryknoll publication. Initially, that publication was *A Field Afar* made famous by the first generation of Maryknoll men and women who produced it. Now called *The Maryknoll Mission Magazine* with its Spanish equivalent of *Revista*, Maryknoll Magazine has done the lion's share of work in introducing the Catholic American family to the foreign missions. Its fabulous pictures and personal stories has evoked the spiritual imagination and inspired many to consider mission work as a vocation. It has allowed monetary resources from "the haves" in the world to be passed to direct service projects for those who "have not." Encouraging this stewardship, Maryknoll has served as a vehicle for social justice efforts beyond their own countries.

In addition, Maryknoll's own publishing house, Orbis Press, produces professional and biopic books from authors all over the world who have something to contribute to the mission endeavor of the church. International authors from academics and the social sciences, as well as Maryknoll missionaries, and those who have researched and reflected on the theological challenges of the larger world, have found their work welcomed by Orbis Press. Printed text has been one means utilized effectively by the Maryknoll communities to educate the northern hemisphere about the situations in the missions in the southern hemisphere.

Maryknoll Spirituality

In addition to the hardcopy of the magazines, Maryknoll missionaries spend ample time with mission appeals in parishes, telling their stories. They send out Mission Awareness teams to schools and interest groups to keep alive the story of the mission experience. Sisters are required to give home service to keep reverse mission going so that the stories are not lost. Their experiences abroad are essential for conveying a broader awareness of the socio-political realities often overlooked in national news.

Respect for Cultural Diversity

As early as the 1920s, when the initial steps of Maryknoll missionaries had been placed in China, Korea, the Philippines, Hong Kong, Manchuria, and Hawaii, Maryknoll founders were stretching their congregations to embrace respectfully the cultures in which they were ministering. Before inculturation was a term endorsed by the Second Vatican Council in the mid 1960s, Maryknoll missionaries were already settling into customs and lifestyles that were foreign to them, but familiar to those in their host countries. A stroll down the halls of the Knoll in Ossining, New York, reveals the diversity and appreciation they acquired for the art, the clothing, and the beauty they met in these places. While their American roots cannot be downplayed, Maryknoll missionaries have spent ample time, money, and mental energy in passing over into these cultures to understand the underlying perspectives that govern the way of life. This flexibility that was encouraged in their charism has resulted in a rich treasury of insight and regard for all peoples throughout the world and the spiritual heritage that makes up these cultures.

Direct Service Opportunities

Many religious communities in this millennium now have associates programs that allow them to nurture the interest in their charism, but Maryknoll championed this development through their support of short-term lay missionaries and associates, who felt drawn to offer some years of their lives to international service. Since language is a concern in any mission field, lay missionaries are required to give at least a three-year commitment in addition to a formation period of training as missionaries. This initial volunteer experience has crystallized into a new arm of

Part IV: Missionary Spirituality

the Maryknoll family in the development of the Maryknoll Lay Missioner Association. Initially under the governance of the Maryknoll Fathers and Brothers, the Maryknoll laity now have administrative autonomy, but continue to work alongside the religious in various mission territories. These men and women bring marriage and family directly into the Maryknoll community, modeling abroad an affirmation of the healthy, holy Christian domestic church.

In Summary

The broad family of Maryknoll covers women religious, priests, brothers, and laity who all seek to promote equity of resources and expansion of Christian values in the world. An approach of presence and pastoral practice jointly fuels the Maryknoll mission. Their missionaries have been involved in all strata of society and pastoral work within the multitude of nations to which they have been missioned. Their pastoral involvement has led them to contribute to the fields of education, economic development, health care, social services, and peace and justice ministry. Their ministry also includes work with refugees and migrants, women, and indigenous religious.

The Maryknoll sisters have tried to stress the incorporation of a contemplative dimension to their spiritual lives, too, to complement the active element of their charism. They have emphasized raising up the local church and working themselves out of their jobs. This empowerment is a feature of Maryknoll spirituality that keeps them respectful of other communities' needs and strengths. A microcosm of the larger world, Maryknoll sisters, brothers, priests, and laity accompany others wherever the needs emerge and they are stretched in their own mission identity, even as they stretch the awareness of those at home and abroad.

Questions for Reflection:

- Does the martyr symbol hold any meaning for you? Have you ever known a martyr?
- Have you ever felt drawn to leave family behind to minister in a foreign land?

Resources for Ongoing Study:

Catholic Foreign Mission Society of America. *Maryknoll—A Journey of Faith*, Maryknoll, NY: Maryknoll Fathers and Brothers, 1996.

Kennedy, Camilla. *To the Uttermost Parts of the Earth: The Spirit and Charism of Mary Josephine Rogers*. Maryknoll, NY: Maryknoll, 1987.

Marie, Sister Jeanne. *Maryknoll's First Lady*. New York: Dodd Mead, 1964.

13

Spirituality of the Society of African Missions
Dedication to Africa

VERY FEW PEOPLE HAVE heard of the Society of African Missions, which originated in France in 1856. The men and now women who work in this canonical society of priests and lay associates are missioned most to Africa to meet the needs of the church and populace there. Africa is where the resources of personnel and finances are sent. Though small in number, this community has a mighty energy of dedication and devotion specifically to the vast African continent. Let us pause here to see the legacy of this intrepid group of missionaries.

Milieu

The mission thrust of the mid-1800s sent brave Christian servants primarily to the soil of India, Korea, Southeast Asia, and the Americas. Much energy in the revitalized French Church was focused on Indochina, and this fresh momentum was encouraged by powerful popes of the time. But the continent of Africa was one that was only skirted by traders and shipmen who careened around the edges by water. Though there were ancient populations and empires within the massive landmass, few men and women knew of the wealth and history of these people. Their needs were relegated to the side because the obstacles to penetrating the jungles, deserts, and rocky coasts were formidable. Slave traders broached these shores for personal financial gain, but none came near in an attempt to improve the lives and development of the peoples who lived there. East Africa had seen some missionary activity but West and Central Africa was forgotten and neglected. It was only valued for the benefit it could offer colonizers and political expansionists. Then a man dedicated to help it came along in the person of Melchior de Marion Bresillac.

The Founder

Among nineteenth-century founders, what is recorded of Melchior de Marion Bresillac comes from letters and personal writings. Less attention is paid him than many others who founded similar congregations. He was the firstborn of a devout Catholic couple in southern France in December of 1813. Though not a poor family, they had lost their means in the French Revolution and moved frequently to adjust to their loss of income. Melchior was a loner with an early appreciation for religious ritual, constructing his own little "cathedral" where he invited local children to join him in worship. His was a serious nature, reserved, but one loyal to his family and upright in his character. He was educated at home until he went to the minor seminary at eighteen years of age.

Ordained a priest in 1838, he joined the Paris Foreign Missions in 1841 and was sent to India as a missionary. His interest in the education of local clergy gained him the attention of his superiors and he was quickly reassigned to the seminary. Then in 1846 he was named a bishop, despite his desire to be a simple missionary among the indigenous people. By 1849, however, he sought to resign that appointment. A matter of conscience over the Indian caste system, the disorganization of the Paris Foreign Missions, and discontent among his own priests led him to depart from India, saddened and shaken about his future.

Notable in Melchior de Marion Bresillac was the consistent practice unlike many of his day of giving himself to an eight-day silent, directed retreat before major decisions or departures. This exhibited his deep devotion to prayer and structured discernment. He carried this practice to India and back, resorting to deliberate prayer and direction as a facet of his deep spiritual life. This helped him manage his intensity and scrupulosity as he tested his desire for mission and new endeavors. He was committed to do nothing contrary to the glory of God.

With his commitment to mission still intact, he looked for other ways to fulfill his call. Africa was "the most abandoned continent" as missions went. He began to set his mind and heart towards her western coast and interior where no missionaries had successfully set foot. He was offered the mission territory of Sierra Leone in West Africa.

The toll of this brash climate and these harsh conditions was high. The early necrology of the Society of African Missions cites the death of all their young priests to yellow fever, malaria, and cholera within months if not days of landing. The first group of SMA priests departed for Sierra Leone in November of 1858. De Marion Bresillac himself followed four months later and died a young death at 46 years of age, only four months after landing in Freetown. "The White Man's Graveyard" had claimed the first round of missionaries from the Society of African Missions, but they would not be the last to come.

Spiritual Legacy for Today:
To Be a Missionary From the Bottom of His Heart

The spirituality of Melchior de Marion Bresillac was one that firmly embraced the cross and all the sacrifices that went with mission in unkind fields. Fresh inspiration germinated within him for the most abandoned. For these he was willing to sacrifice his life. His legacy incorporated this self-sacrifice with zeal and courage. His commitment to the three theological virtues of faith, hope, and charity propelled him into service and he stalwartly advocated for the raising up of other brave souls within the Society of African Missions and dioceses abroad who could carry the Gospel challenge further. We pause now to reflect on these gifts from his legacy.

Sacrifice, Zeal, and Courage

Radical in his zeal for mission, de Marion Bresillac modeled the sacrificial heart and mind that was needed to sustain the work of mission in unfriendly territories. His courage in proceeding ahead with the call to

Spirituality of the Society of African Missions

mission despite the immediate deaths of his community members encouraged the Society of African Missions to continue despite the loss of their founder. These early missionaries consecrated their lives to what appeared to be a lost cause. They willingly risked death to carry the Gospel to West Africa. As active apostolic missionaries, the SMAs continued to send men with that same zeal and courage and slowly made inroads where no others were able. They were missionaries from the bottom of their hearts.

Faith, Hope, and Charity

The last words that Melchior de Marion Bresillac spoke were, "Faith, hope, and ch—." Yes, charity. These were central principles to the spiritual life and the life of a good missionary. Simple and succinct, these virtues were lived out by those who followed in his footsteps. They were not simple mandates, especially in foreign countries with strange customs and practices. However, they served as the cornerstones for a Christian foundation that would be built on African shores. These essentials were primary in the spirituality of de Marion Bresillac. They shaped the formation of SMA seminarians and lay missionaries, reducing the complexity of mission to the basics of Christian practice and belief. Faith, hope and charity were perennial instructions to each missionary sent out and the first instructions given to the catechumen they met and lead onto the Christian path.

Support of Local Clergy

From de Marion Bresillac's earliest days he had been involved actively with the education of clergy. While in the minor seminary, he had taught mathematics and science. As a young missionary in India, he had taken on the serious responsibilities and challenges of the seminary, advocating for the proper formation of local clergy. This in itself had gained approval of diocesan personnel and landed him in the Pro-Vicariate chair. The idea of raising up a local clergy had been his "heart's desire." In keeping with that concern, the Society of African Missions continued to collaborate with bishops throughout Africa to support the development of a strong local leadership. The SMA Fathers, as they were known, encouraged young men to explore their vocations to serve their home dioceses, often limiting the potential for their own numbers as a missionary congregation to be increased. They provided personnel to seminaries, sponsored diocesan clergy by paying tuition for their studies in Africa and abroad, and formed close personal friendships of support and collegiality with diocesan priests. De Marion Bresillac's devotion to founding a solid foundation for an emerging African Church was honored by his brother SMAs throughout the century and a half since their inception.

Contemporary Spiritual and Pastoral Contributions

The Society of African Missions is a small group by comparison to the Jesuits, Franciscans, and Spiritans. They are relatively unknown. Most of their personnel are in Africa on mission or in studies. They are involved in Christian-Muslim dialogue, seminary formation for clergy, and lay integration in the missions. The contributions they render that are valuable to us today include an endurance for the Gospel despite hardship, a devotion to Africa and her needs, and the offering of personnel as bishops as requested by Rome. We will see how each of these is a gift for us today.

Endurance

Endurance and perseverance are frequently linked with one another. A thesaurus offers us words like fortitude and persistence to explain the capacity to survive when so many odds are against us. The SMA missionaries practice these same virtues in lands where hostility towards Christianity is sometimes still encountered. They are no more herculean than we are, but they go with hearts that are willing to apply the principles of Christian life in countries not their own. Their early founders and followers practiced a muscular endurance that may not be required of contemporary believers. Few of us will face the extreme challenges met by missionaries in Africa, but the endurance and perseverance is still a trait from which we can benefit. As Christians we are stretched frequently in our attempts to practice patience, charity, and good humor. The stamina and staying power evidenced in the priests and lay missionaries of the Society of African Missions can inspire us to face our own struggles and even sacrifice some of our own comforts without retracting into self-protectiveness.

Devotion to Africa

Before it was fashionable or sexy to advocate for Africa, the Society of African Missions did it. Their work all over Africa in villages and remote areas is still a display of their undying affection for the peoples and lands of this phenomenal continent. With pockets that are not so deep, they sink their money and personnel into projects that need undivided attention. They are exclusively fastened to the hip of African people. As an international society of priests and lay missionaries from France, Germany, Ireland, Spain, Italy, the Netherlands, the United State, Argentina, India, Poland, the Philippines, England, and Africa itself, the Society continues to pump energy and ideas into the evangelization of Africa. They are shaped by that encounter themselves as new missionaries come forth from the African community to join them in their work. They listen as the voice of new African theologians begins to emerge. They want to be there to hear them speak, to hear the new spin on Christianity as it is articulated from an African cultural perspective.

While they work on African soil, they also advocate for the needs of Africa among the educated and powerful in Europe and the United States. They challenge the budgets of these countries and appeal through official entities like the Africa Faith and Justice Network for a sharing of the pie. They keep on the front burner the concerns and the critical needs of a continent that was once most abandoned.

Bishops

From a cynical perspective we may be hesitant to name bishops as a valuable contribution by a missionary society, but many dioceses in Africa are the beneficiaries of initial church leadership under the guidance of former SMA priests. With a long history of involvement in the mission fields, these SMA bishops bring with them a devotion and knowledge of those they are called to lead. Some of them bring an awareness of the structure of the Church in Rome that helps budding dioceses begin to stabilize themselves. In addition they bring contacts with parishes and dioceses in the northern hemisphere that can be approached to help finance projects and buildings in areas where no funds are readily available. Many of these SMA bishops assume leadership tentatively, seeing themselves as temporary until African personnel are ready. They are willing to work themselves out of a job as soon as they can, leaving the future of the African church soundly in the hands of adept and able African leaders.

In Summary

We conclude this final chapter on missionary schools of spirituality with the amazing story of the Society of African Missions. Slowly and happily, this community sees the fruit of its 150 years of ministry blossoming in the vocations coming out of Africa. They have nurtured local clergy and received many earnest missionaries themselves into their own fold. In addition they have spent energy and time encouraging lay missionaries to join them in the work with children, refugees, lepers, and catechumen all over the continent. They continue to educate seminarians in houses of formation in both West and East Africa, letting their presence contribute to the livelihood of the Church of the future. They have withstood civil war in Liberia and Sierra Leone, inter-religious violence in Nigeria, post-election rebellion in Kenya, economic crises in Zambia, and massive dislocation of populations of refugees in Ghana and Ivory Coast. These are only a fraction of the challenges they face as a congregation. By their very existence, they invite us to reconsider our own response to the needs of Africa. They shall continue to do so until they have worked themselves completely out of the job.

Questions for Reflection:

- Have you ever felt compelled to explore Africa and meet her peoples?
- Do you know any missionaries? What has impressed you about their persons or their work?

Resources for Ongoing Study:

O'Shea, Michael. *Mission or Martyrdom? The Spirituality of Melchior de Marion Bresillac and the Society of African Missions.* Ibadan: John-Mof Printers, 1989.

The Call of Africa. Tenafly: The Society of African Missions American Province, 1941.

Epilogue

As we have seen in these pages, many souls throughout history have vibrated with enthusiasm for the word of God. They have been awakened by the Holy Spirit to the ancient message of Christ. Seized by this new and personal awareness of God and the Gospel, they have responded wholeheartedly to the summons to act. In the cases of these charismatic founders and foundresses new life and fresh creativity came into the church.

Let us stop and think for a moment about the number and names of the gifts we have been given from within these traditions through their legacies and their spiritual and pastoral contributions. We have named over eighty! A quick review may help us appreciate the vast treasure that we have. While these gifts have been attributed primarily to one of the communities described in this book, none of them is the exclusive domain of any one group. Many of the contributions named are evident in a significant number of other communities, evidence that the Holy Spirit is generous in bestowing her gifts and graces.

Under the umbrella of the monastic school of spirituality we feature three spiritual communities: Augustinian, Benedictine, and Cistercian or Trappist. We are blessed with riches from the Augustinian legacy of caritas or love, specifically in relationship to God and the world. The emphasis of this school of spirituality on the Trinity and the encouragement to develop a personal, passionate relationship with God promises potential transformation of the world. Augustinian spirituality bequeaths to us the spiritual autobiography of Augustine, a model for our own reflection on our spiritual formation stories. The emphasis on the conversion process as a gradual one that develops love and forgiveness as Christian virtues is a comfort and challenge to us as contemporary practitioners.

Epilogue

The school of spirituality of the Benedictines offers us guidance for ordering our lives. Their legacy as monastics is one of community, moderation, obedience, and vocal prayer as means to deepen our spiritual lives. Concretely, they contribute tools for deepening our prayer life with the methods of Lectio Divina and the liturgy of the hours. The rhythm of monastic life itself still serves as a model of the ordered way of balancing work, study, and prayer.

The Cistercian and Trappist spiritual legacy emphasizes silence and stillness as a means to personal holiness. Their collegial governance provides a structure for communal life and a method of decision-making that has served as models for subsequent religious communities the world over. This form of governance through a "chapter" of leaders has allowed generations of religious to maintain unity within autonomy. The contribution of this school of spirituality to us as contemporary seekers includes the personal autobiographical example of Thomas Merton, a monk of the twentieth century who from his monastic home wrote integrative challenges about the transformation of self and world through spiritual development. Merton continues to have a following of readers who apply his instructions and wisdom to their personal and political involvement in the world.

The second umbrella of spirituality in our text is the mendicant school, which is modeled by the three communities of the Franciscans, the Dominicans, and the Carmelites. The Franciscan school of spirituality brings a broad, inclusive spirituality of complete dependence on God, one that can renew the church and inform contemporary missionaries. Francis' dedication to serving the poor is a centerpiece of his legacy and his devotion to Christ inspires the building of Christmas crèches still to this day. The contributions of this tradition to contemporary believers are radical Gospel simplicity, ecological reverence, and hospitality, all of which stretch us to become more committed to the message of Christ expressed in preservation of creation and welcome of strangers.

While the Franciscan school fosters a spirituality of the heart, the mendicant school of the Dominicans offers a spirituality of the head. This legacy that encourages study and the pursuit of truth counterbalances the affective form of Franciscan spirituality. Dominican spirituality emphasizes the salvation of all and stresses the necessity of study to educate people about their faith. For us as contemporary believers the Dominican school places value on the intellect in the spiritual life and leaves behind a rich trove of theological and spiritual writings from geniuses like St. Thomas Aquinas, Catherine of Siena, and Meister Eckhart. The Dominican school also bequeaths a new democratic religious structure, opening the doors of the monastic world and releasing its members to a larger region of service and availability.

Third in our examination of the mendicant school of spirituality is the Carmelite community, whose spiritual legacy is decidedly contemplative and focused on a love that leads to union with God. The singlemindedness and solitude of contemplative mystics from within this tradition is a fabulous resource. The blend of mendicancy in a contemplative communal life is an unusual one, but one that walks shoeless or discalced between the monastic and the world. A gift from this tradition is the brown scapular, a small felt neckpiece worn under clothing as a constant reminder of Mary's promise that salvation will be granted to those who willingly submit to God's plan. Finally, the contemporary contributions for us today include poetry, especially that of John of the Cross, the mystical metaphors of the many Carmelite writers, the gutsy self-awareness in the spiritual life with no egoistic illusion, and the ever-necessary call to prayer.

A third umbrella school of spirituality in this text is that of the ministerial and active apostolic traditions. Four are featured in our text, namely the Jesuit, Redemptorist, Salesian, and Marist communities. The overarching gift of these four religious communities is a spirituality that propels us into the streets to serve directly the needs of others as a central expression of our vocational and spiritual lives.

Jesuit or Ignatian spirituality is described as a unique apostolic spirituality that embeds us in a world of action, recognizing God within the activity. Discernment of life choices for their consonance with the Christian call is a part of the legacy of Ignatius. The transformation of institutions and individuals is a focal point of expression for this blend of active and contemplative vocation and a spiritual life of direct communication with God, encouraging the use of imagination and reflection in prayer. Tools for us to grow in our spiritual lives today include the examen of consciousness, the directed retreat, and the thirty day exercises of St. Ignatius.

Redemptorist or Alphonsian spirituality brings an awareness of the unconditional love of God and the redeeming act of Jesus Christ as savior. The Redemptorist community encourages the spread of domestic

Epilogue

missions to foster spiritual development at home. Their practical piety is reflected in resources they develop for the common person through publishing materials and evangelizing endeavors. We benefit from the publications that they offer us to further our spiritual lives and deepen our commitment to Christ.

The Salesian spiritual legacy is a spirituality of the heart, using language of the heart to enhance the devout life. Practicing a life of humility is central to this form of spirituality. Evident in the writings of their founders is an openness to Christian humanism, a valuing of the human being, and a responsiveness to her needs. This tradition contributes to the area of spiritual direction and advocates for holiness for the laity. It gives us rich examples of mutual spiritual friendship shared between women and men, even celibates.

Finally, within the active ministerial schools of spirituality we covered is the Marist family. Their legacy, specifically Marian in its focus, emphasizes a collaboration among laity and religious on behalf of the marginalized. The social thrust of this community articulates and addresses the needs of the times, modeling a reformulation of the church under the guidance of Mary. Viewing their work as a continuation of Mary's work in the world, they emphasize inclusivity of the laity, mercy, and compassion.

Our final umbrella school of spirituality is that of missionary communities, which devote themselves to evangelization beyond their home borders. Three communities were our focus: the Spiritans or Holy Ghost Congregation, the Maryknoll missionaries, and the Society of African Missionaries (S.M.A. Fathers).

As their name indicates, the spiritual legacy of the Spiritans centers around the Holy Spirit with a call to evangelical availability and evangelical poverty. Like many missionary communities, they see themselves going where others will not go. As their name indicates, there is an emphasis on the Holy Spirit in these encounters. There is a value placed on experience, flexibility, and personal dignity in this tradition. The Spiritans also contribute a new form of democratic leadership with which contemporary communities can conduct their affairs.

Maryknoll missionaries are the uniquely American community upon which we reflected. While martyrdom is not exclusive to them, many of their members have suffered the ultimate sacrifice in their direct service of the poor. Their missionaries often find themselves in harm's way as they place themselves in countries beyond their home nations. Their active engagement with unjust systems as they try to alleviate inequities and help develop the peoples of mission lands allows them to identify with the needy and promote justice as a community. They contribute significantly to American awareness of the missions, and they spread a respect for cultural diversity and customs in reverse mission work. In addition, mission-minded laypeople can join in direct service as lay missionaries, working alongside seasoned religious and clergy, who are a part of the mission family.

Finally, we looked at the sacrifice, zeal and courage exhibited in a community specifically dedicated to the African continent, the Society of African Missions. Their emphasis on the practice of faith, hope and love along with their support of local clergy is a part of their special legacy. They contribute to ongoing pastoral development through their example of endurance in difficult times and their willingness to allow experienced SMA priests to assume roles as bishops while the indigenous leaders are prepared. They encourage lay missionaries also to join them in their work and in new endeavors that will better the lives of people throughout Africa.

There is an embarrassment of riches placed before us as we review the legacy of these congregations and the ongoing spiritual and pastoral contributions that they bring. The diversity as well as the range of these offerings is somewhat staggering. Think of what we as present-day believers have gained as a result of this panoply of stories, witnesses, and charisms! Without the concretization of the inspiration that prompted these mighty men and women to go forth and "preach" the message of Christ, we would lack the breadth and flexibility of possibilities for expression today. These witnesses have continued the story of Christianity by telling their story of fascination with God. Because they were so courageous, we have a broad array of communities that can teach us and help us frame our own stories.

Each of these founders and foundresses responded to a need in their time. Their energy and zeal crystallized in a form of spirituality that attracted others. This attraction formalized itself into a school that could keep the energy going beyond the limits of that original life that spawned it. Their exuberance gradually attracted like-minded believers to share their vision. They created new structures and avenues for spiritual growth

Epilogue

and their original fire for God resulted in the formation of many religious communities, orders, and societies that addressed the issues of their day.

We are incredibly grateful for this generosity and modeling. We lean on them as wise ones, whose fervor has placed challenges before us. Will we continue to tell the story? Will we have the courage ourselves to listen to the Spirit and respond wholeheartedly? Our stories are the bridges that carry the insight and inspiration of these faithful ones from the past on to the next generation. Our stories will be added to these and provide further encouragement for those coming afterwards. Our own zeal may be the flash of the Spirit needed at this time to address the needs of the current age.

These four schools of spirituality continue to meet a need in our times. New schools of spirituality may be needed for the peculiar challenges of the twenty-first century. But the wisdom shown by these men and women who have given of their lives that we, too, might have faith is something we can depend on. The foundation is strong. Perhaps among us now are new geniuses who can carry the message afresh into new forms that will adapt and extend the Christian story to those who walk ahead.

It is an awe-inspiring movement to be a part of, this Christian story. It is our challenge to reflect on what we are called to do to spread the Good News. Nestled in among us, growing quietly, are the seeds of the next germination of faith. It is possible that among us now future founders and foundresses are being groomed. Their delight in God and our own passion may be the mix that will bring forth new schools to teach the next generation and carry on the enduring and endearing passion of God.

There is still a fire to be cultivated, still hearts to be set ablaze. The energy and vitality of Christianity is a perennial one. Each generation needs to tend that flame. Let us hope the original fire that sparked in previous generation finds new wicks to be enflamed in our's. May the fire be passed on so that our generation and subsequent ones know the warmth and light of Gospel hope.

www.ingramcontent.com/pod-product-compliance
Lightning Source LLC
Chambersburg PA
CBHW022130160426
43197CB00009B/I218